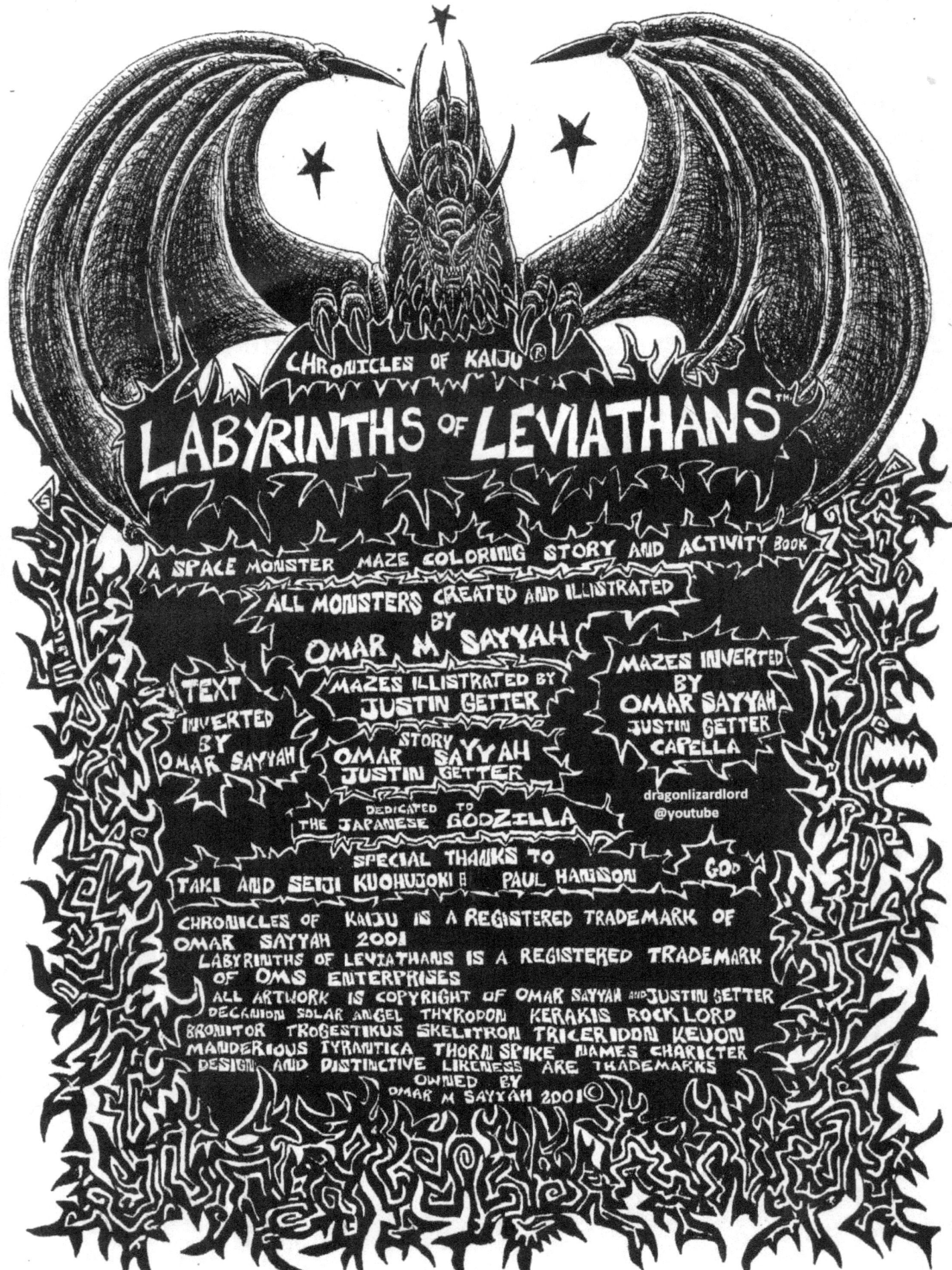

CHRONICLES OF KAIJU®
LABYRINTHS OF LEVIATHANS™

A SPACE MONSTER MAZE COLORING STORY AND ACTIVITY BOOK

ALL MONSTERS CREATED AND ILLUSTRATED
BY
OMAR M SAYYAH

TEXT INVERTED BY OMAR SAYYAH

MAZES ILLUSTRATED BY JUSTIN GETTER

MAZES INVERTED BY OMAR SAYYAH JUSTIN GETTER CAPELLA

STORY
OMAR SAYYAH
JUSTIN GETTER

dragonlizardlord @youtube

DEDICATED TO THE JAPANESE GODZILLA

SPECIAL THANKS TO
TAKI AND SEIJI KUOHUJOKI   PAUL HARRISON   GOD

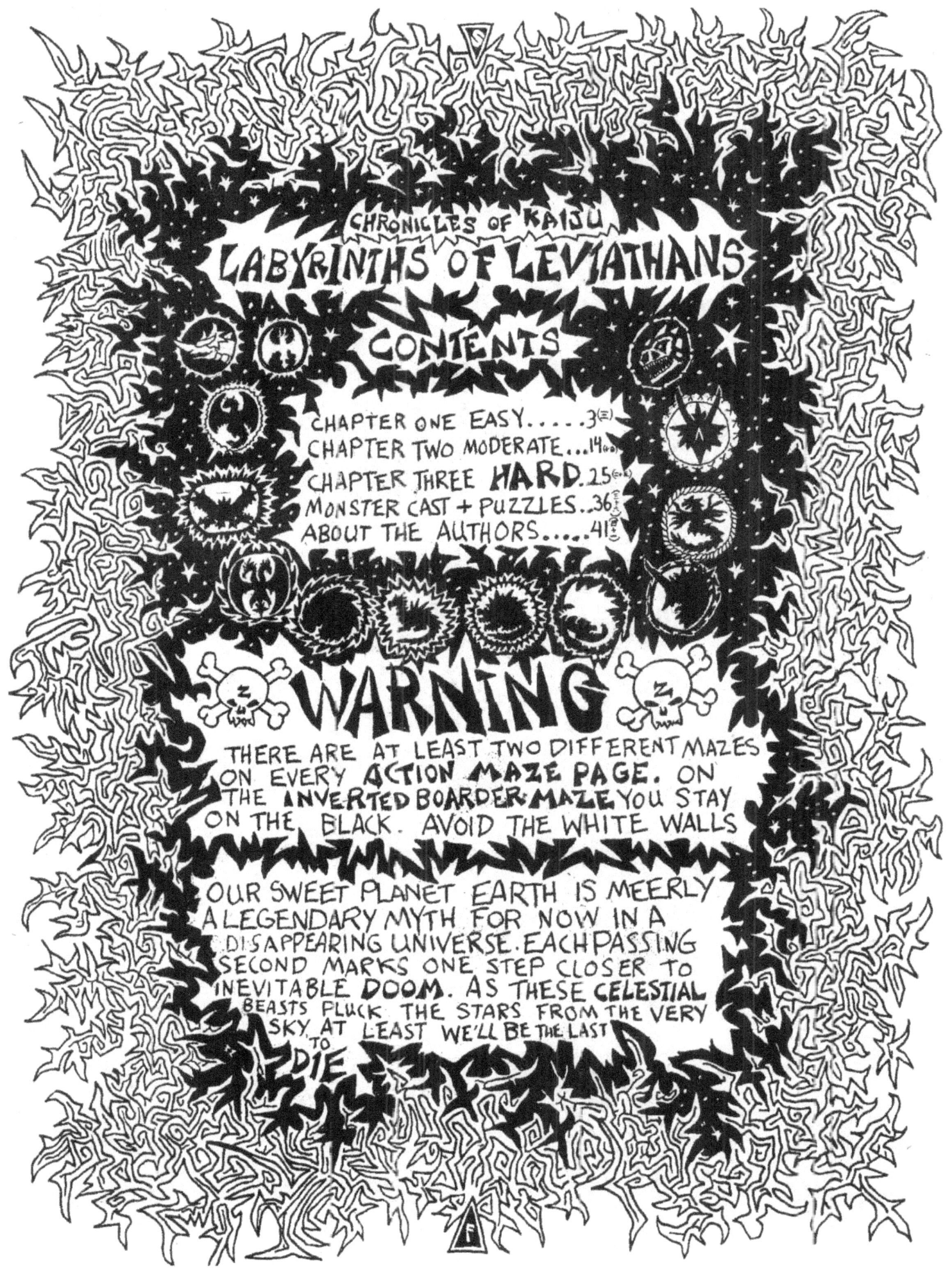

CHRONICLES OF KAIJU
LABYRINTHS OF LEVIATHANS

CONTENTS

WARNING

THERE ARE AT LEAST TWO DIFFERENT MAZES ON EVERY **ACTION MAZE PAGE**. ON THE **INVERTED BOARDER MAZE** YOU STAY ON THE BLACK. AVOID THE WHITE WALLS

OUR SWEET PLANET EARTH IS MEERLY A LEGENDARY MYTH FOR NOW IN A DISAPPEARING UNIVERSE. EACH PASSING SECOND MARKS ONE STEP CLOSER TO INEVITABLE **DOOM**. AS THESE **CELESTIAL** BEASTS PLUCK THE STARS FROM THE VERY SKY AT LEAST WE'LL BE THE LAST TO **DIE**

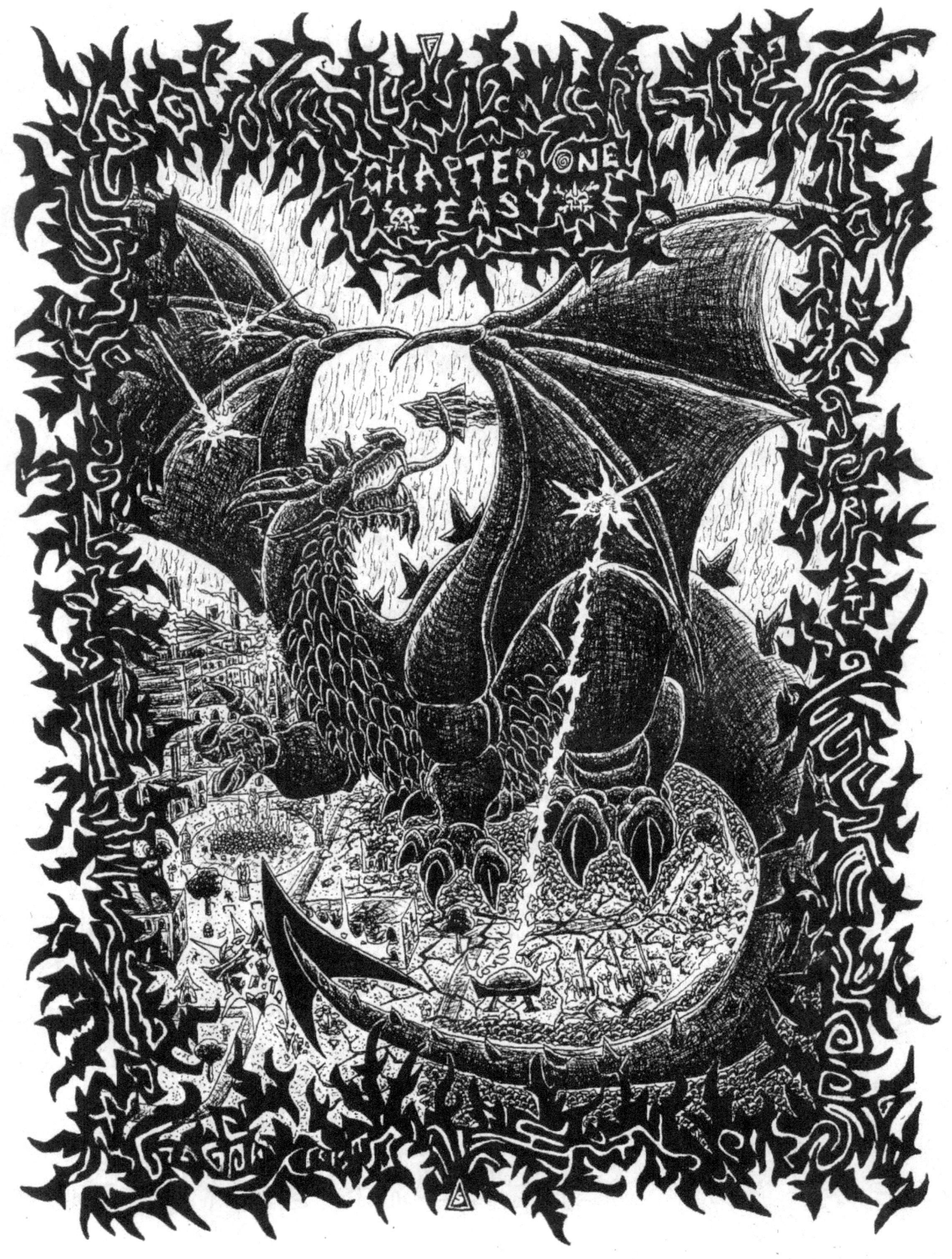

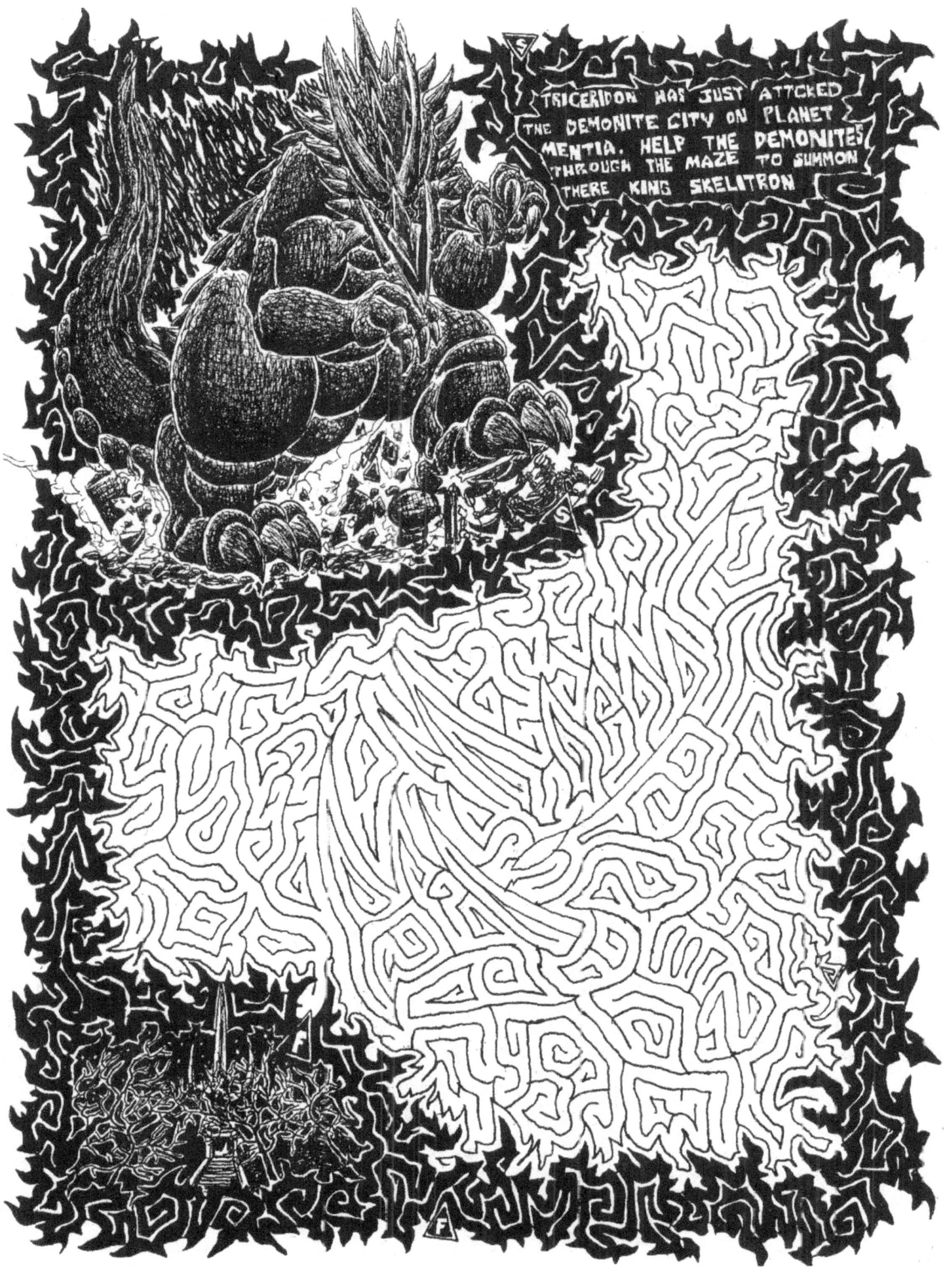

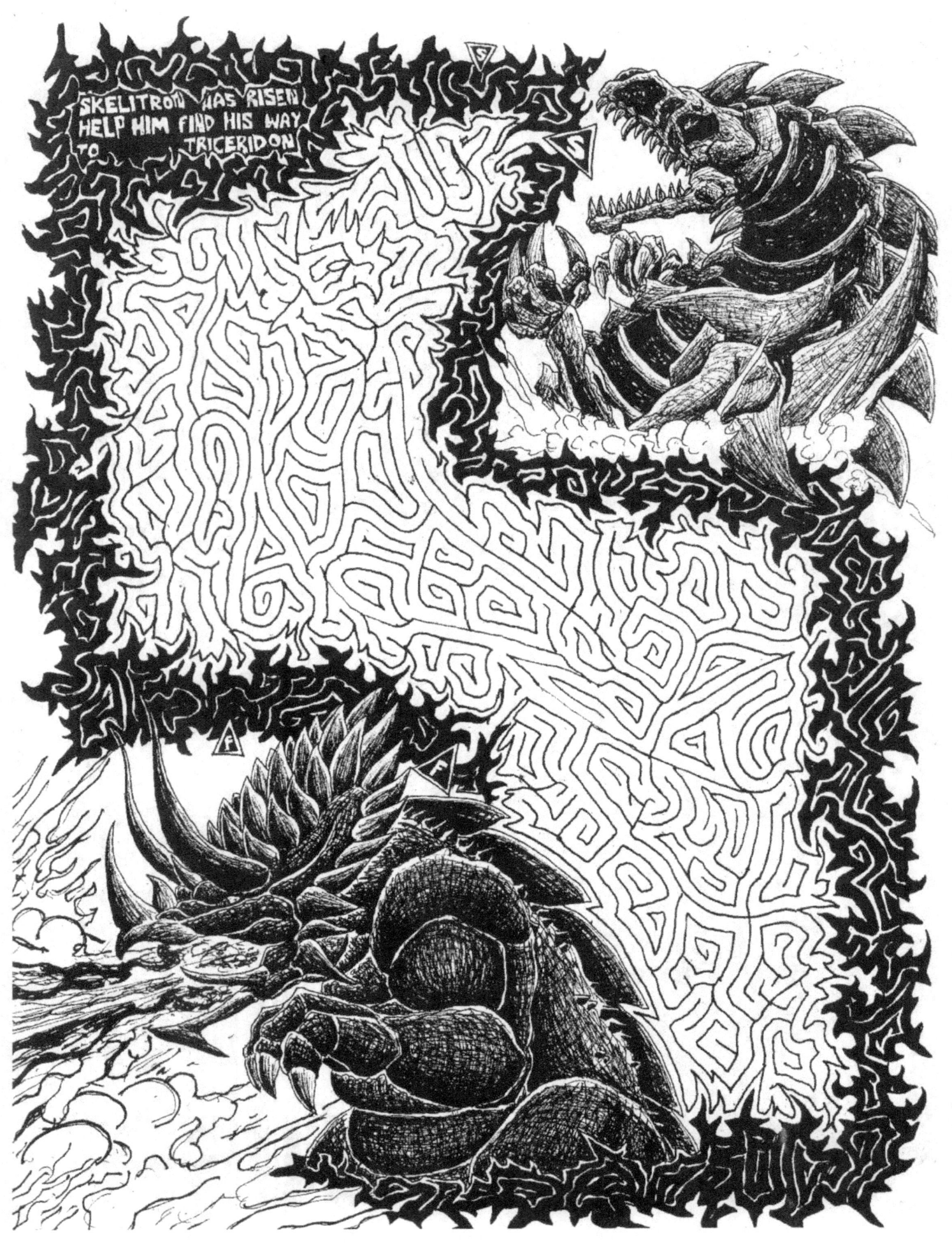

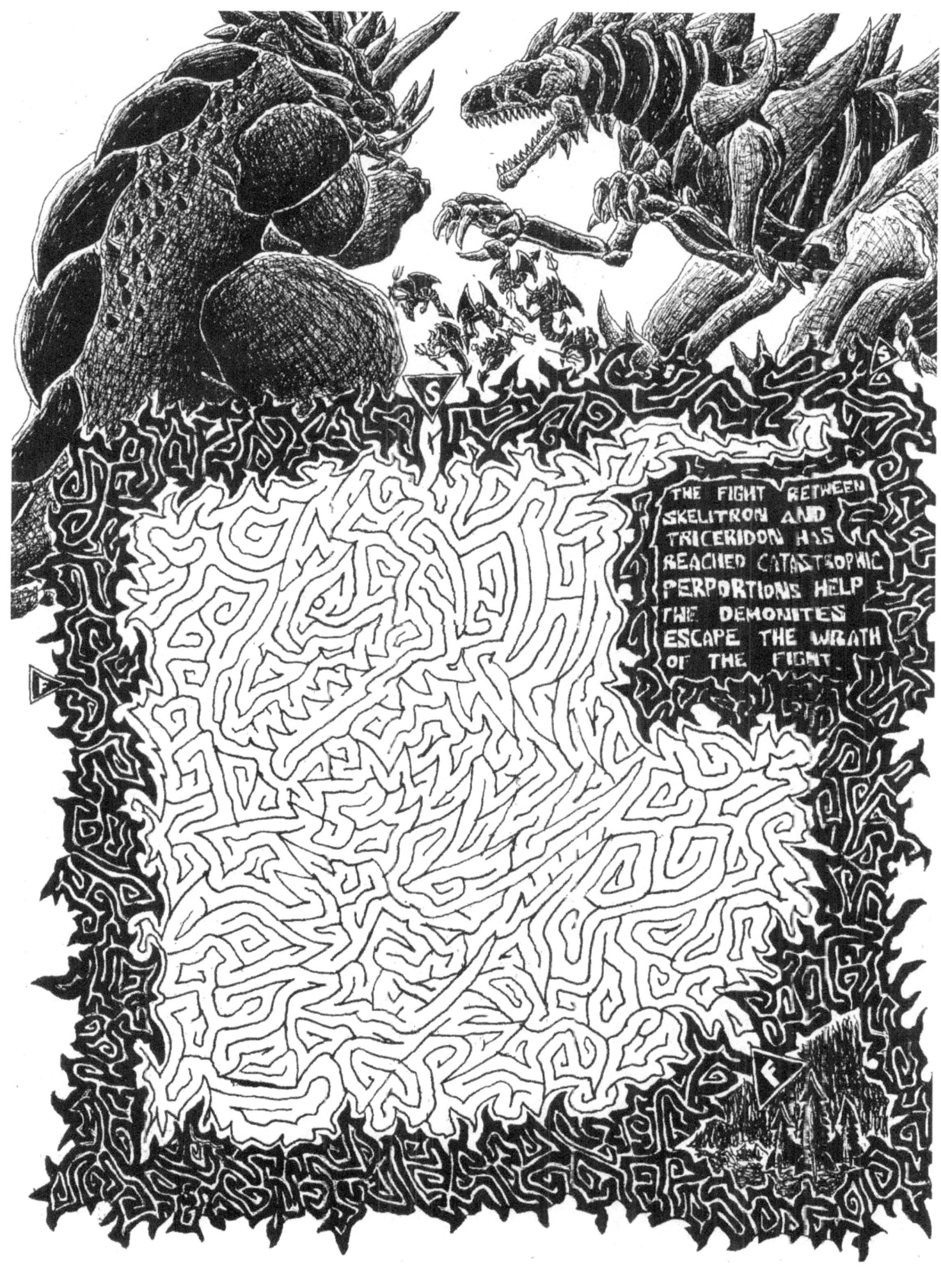

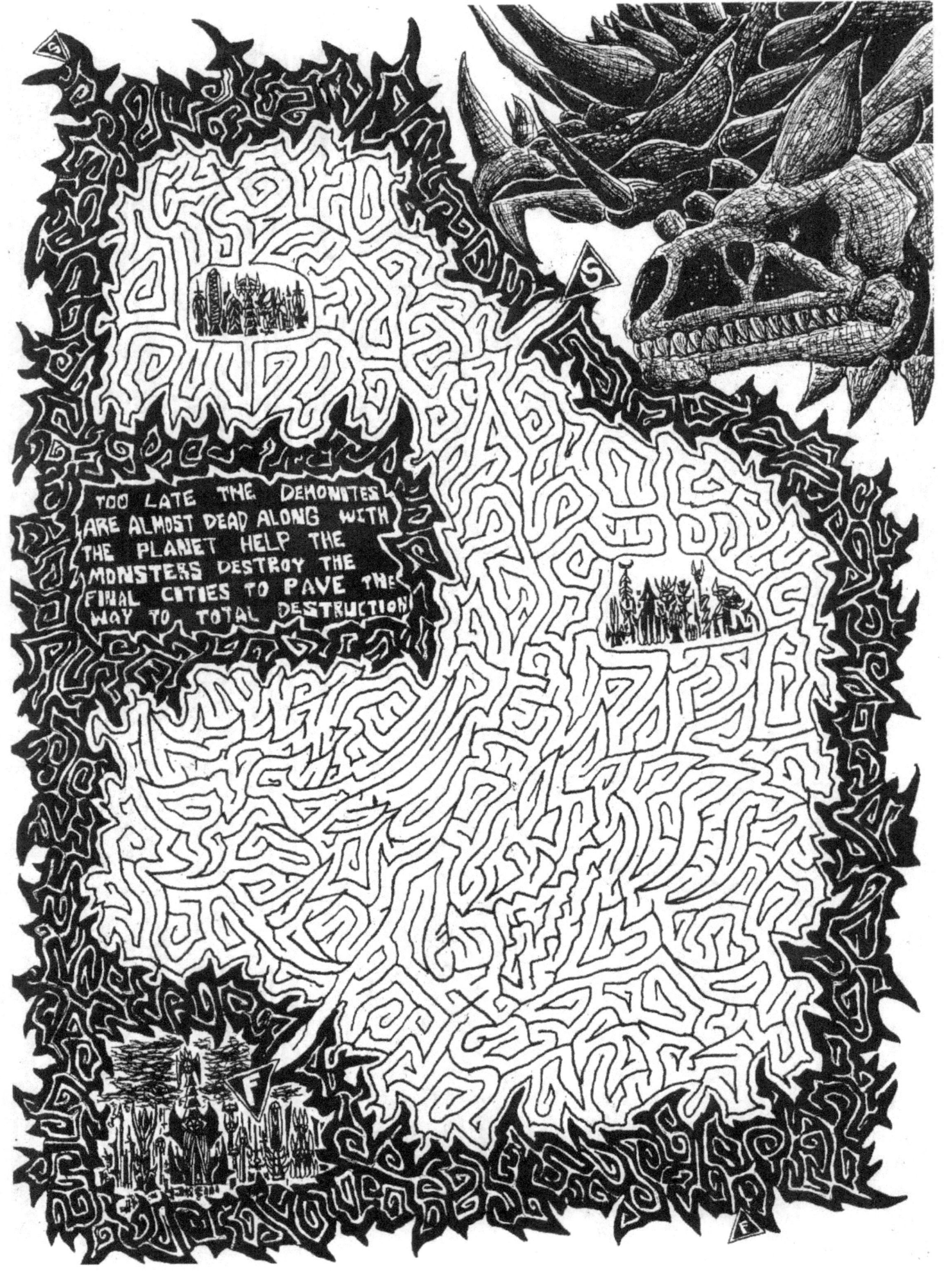

TOO LATE THE DEMONITES ARE ALMOST DEAD ALONG WITH THE PLANET HELP THE MONSTERS DESTROY THE FINAL CITIES TO PAVE THE WAY TO TOTAL DESTRUCTION!

L

JUSTIN GETTER

OMAR SAYYAH

LABYRINTHS OF LEVIATHANS
TIAMATZILLA
DRAGON KING OF THE NORTH SEA
MAZE AND COLORING

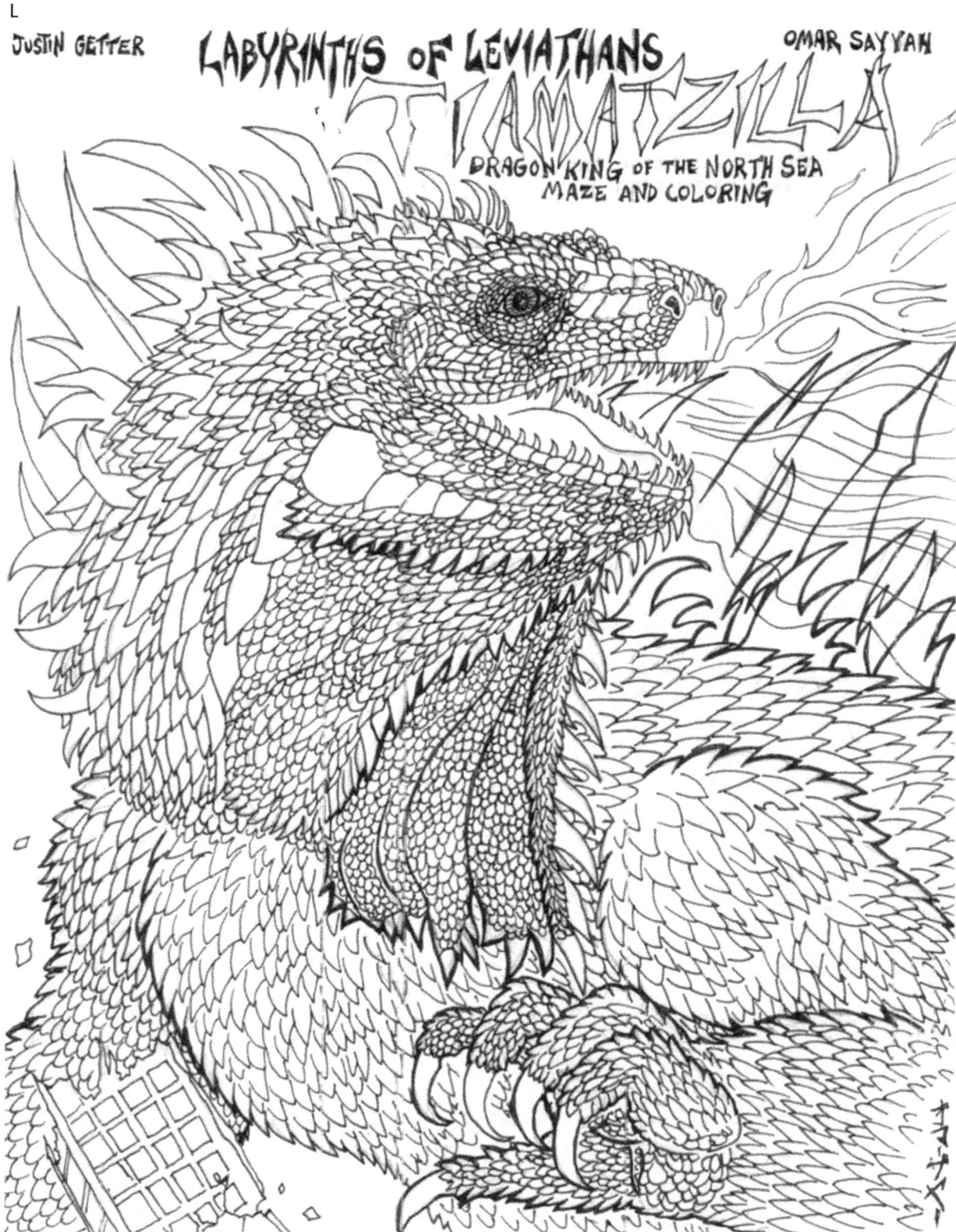

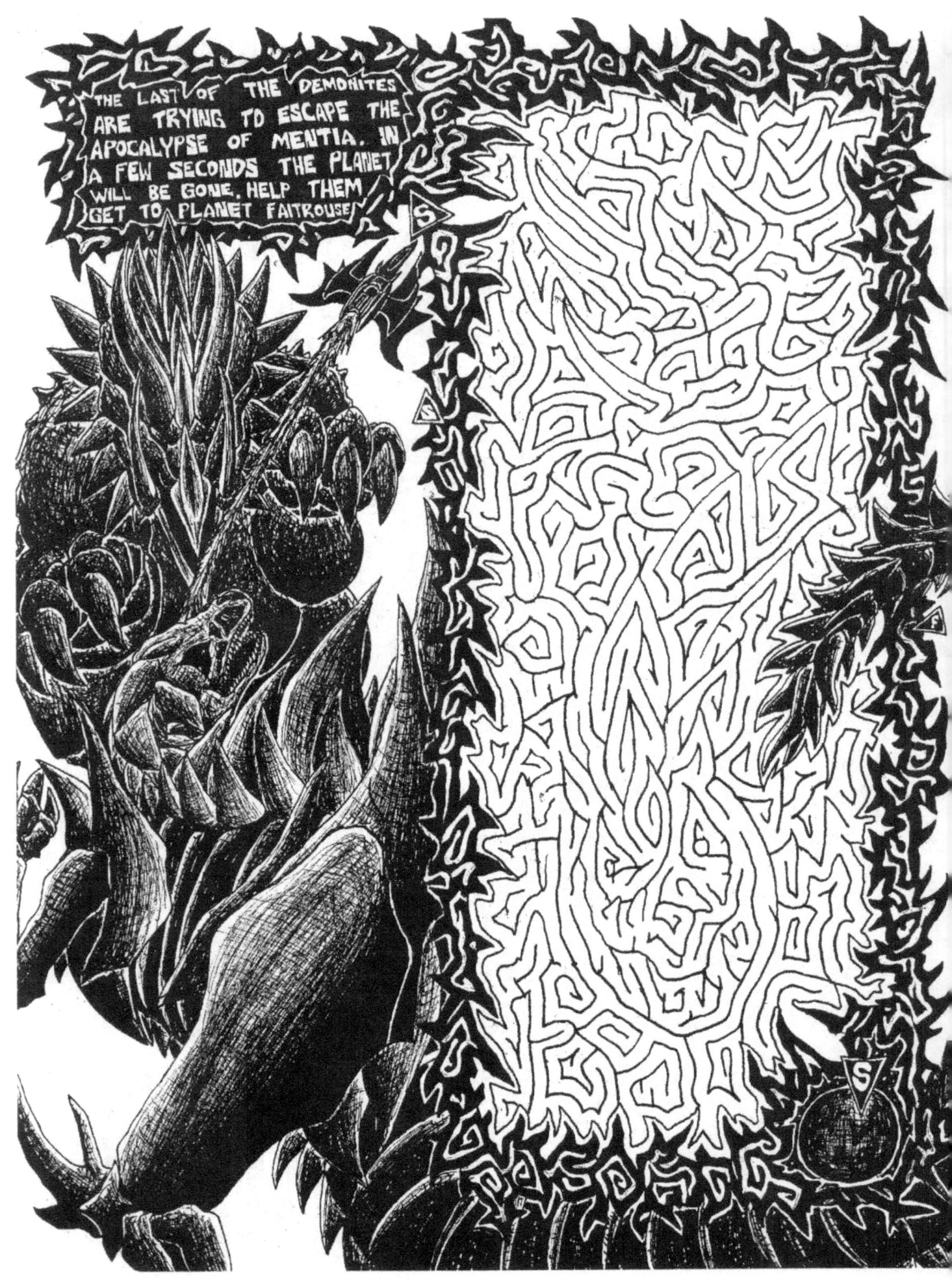

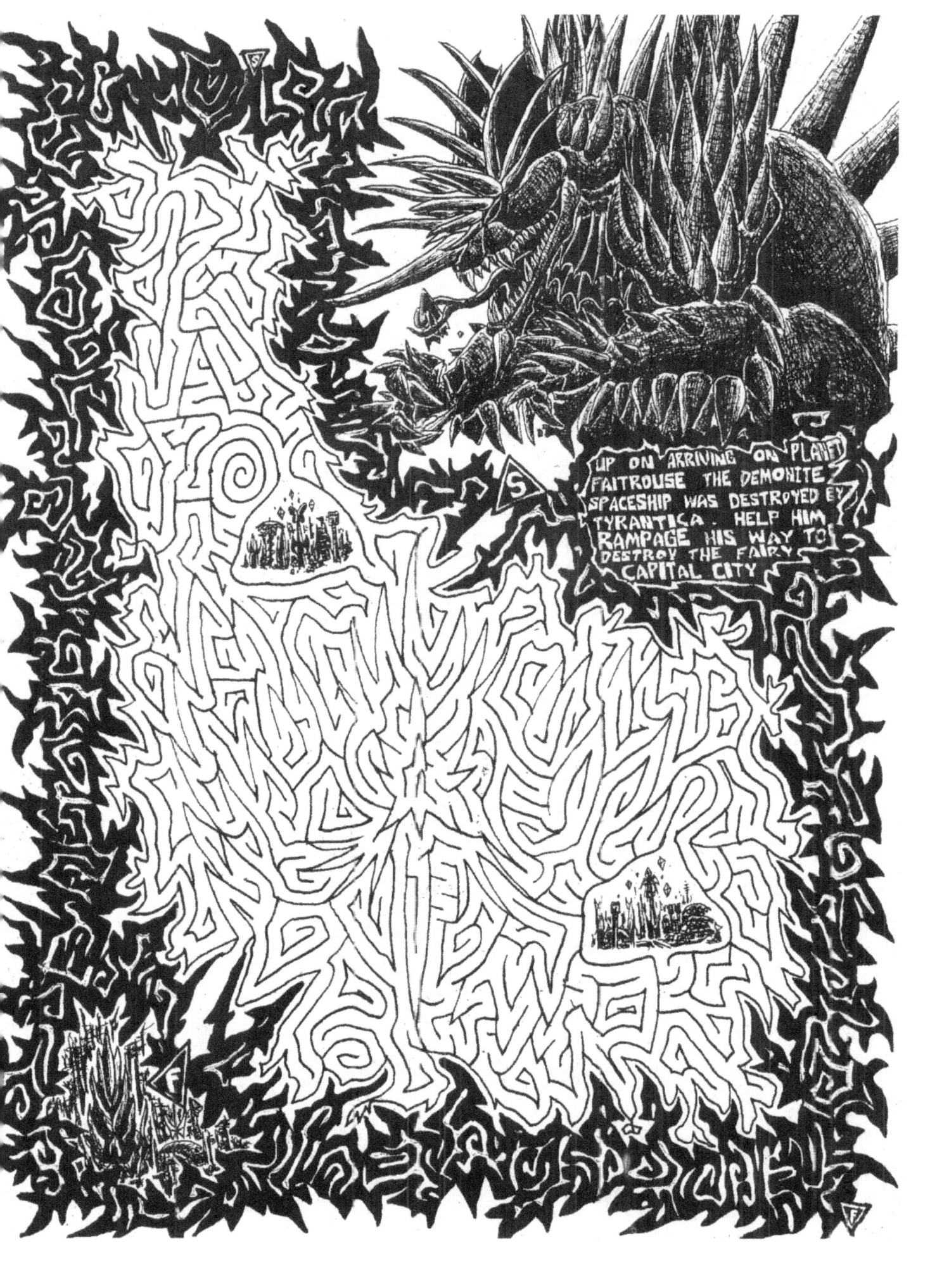

UP ON ARRIVING ON PLANET FAITROUSE THE DEMONITE SPACESHIP WAS DESTROYED BY TYRANTICA. HELP HIM RAMPAGE HIS WAY TO DESTROY THE FAIRY CAPITAL CITY

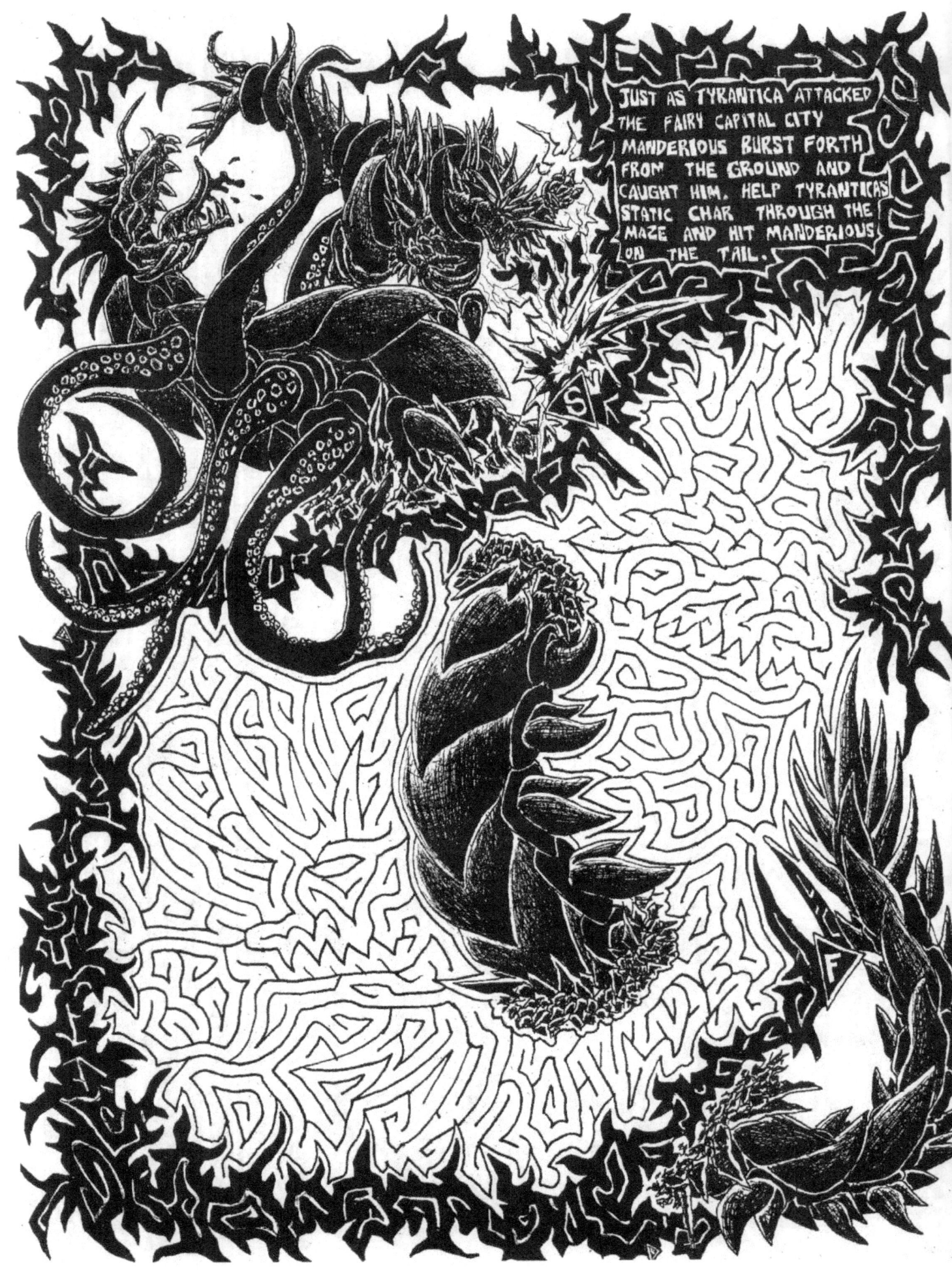

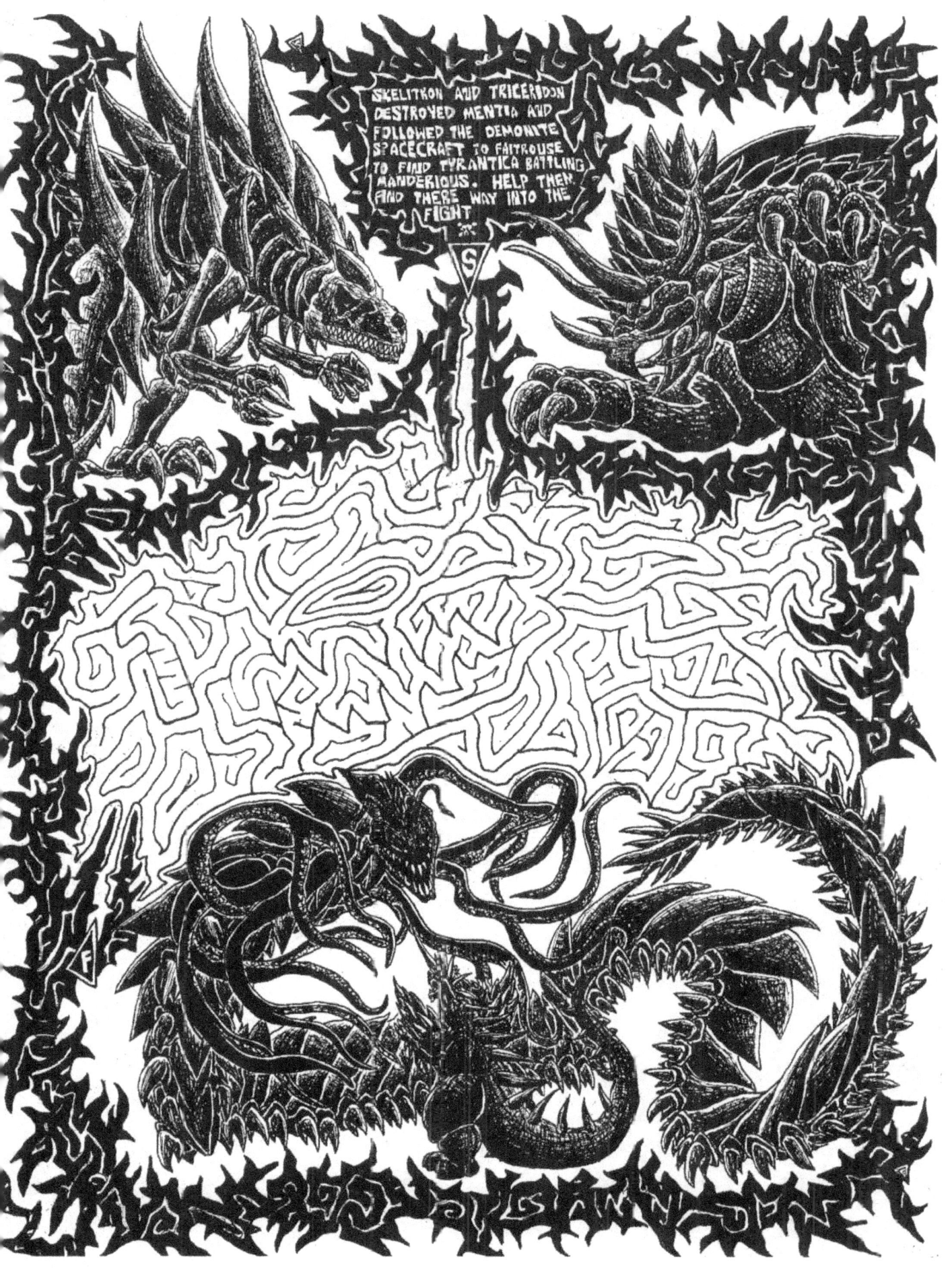

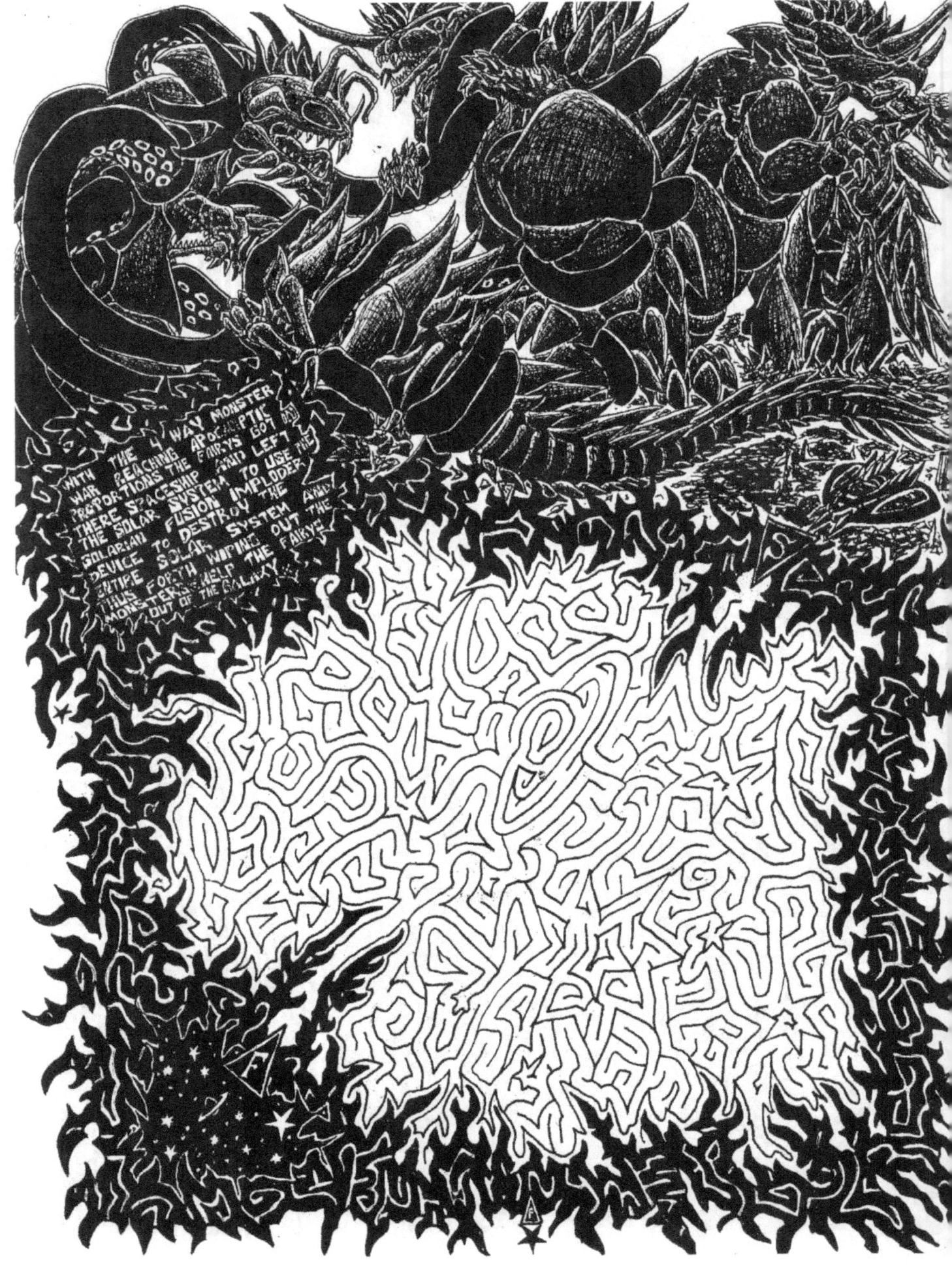

WITH THE 4 WAY MONSTER WAR REACHING APOCALYPTIC PROPORTIONS THE FAIRYS GOT ON THERE SPACESHIP AND LEFT THE SOLAR SYSTEM TO USE THE SOLARIAN FUSION IMPLODER DEVICE TO DESTROY THE ENTIRE SOLAR SYSTEM THUS FORTH WIPING OUT THE MONSTERS! HELP THE FAIRYS OUT OF THE GALAXY !!

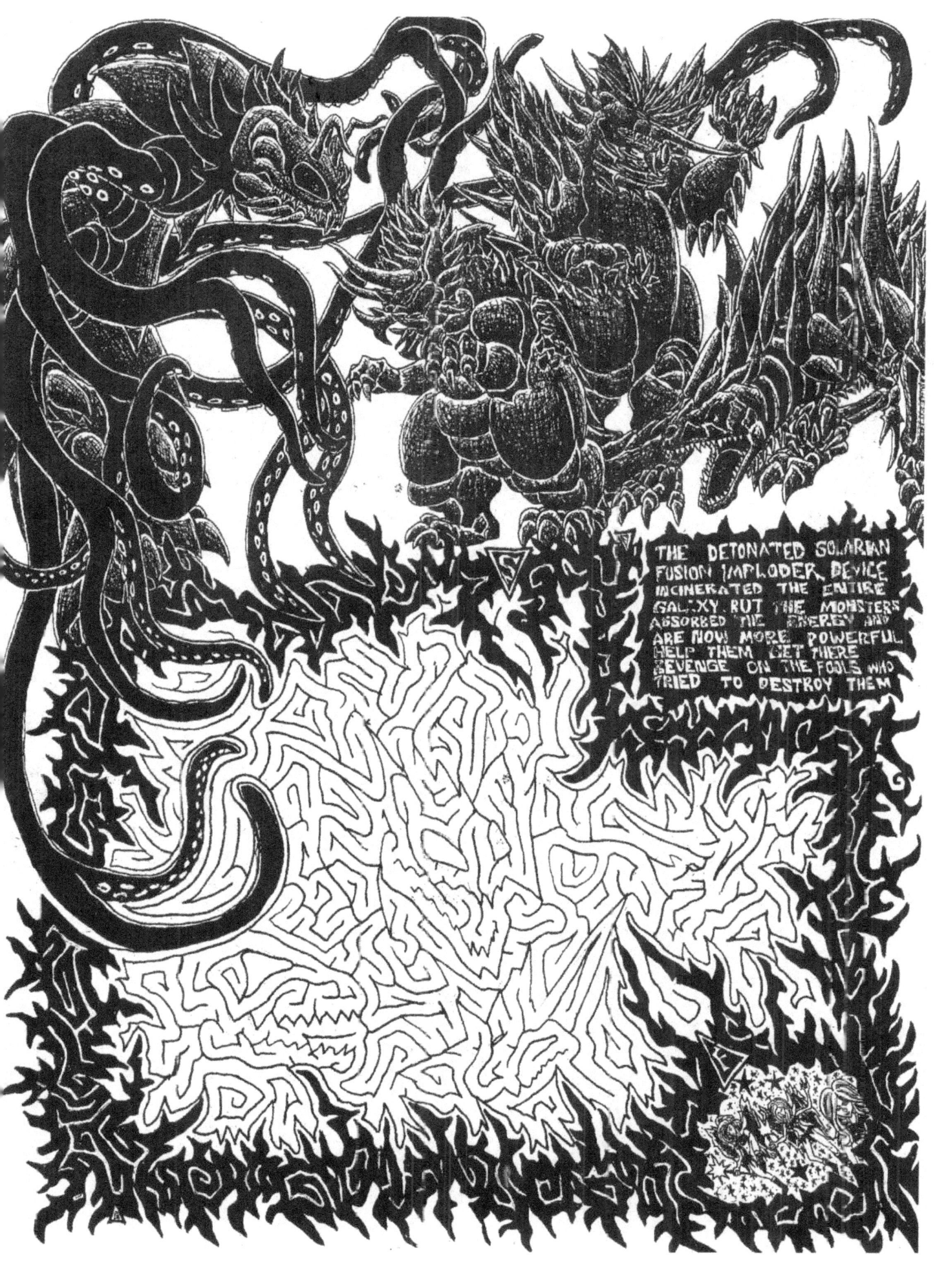

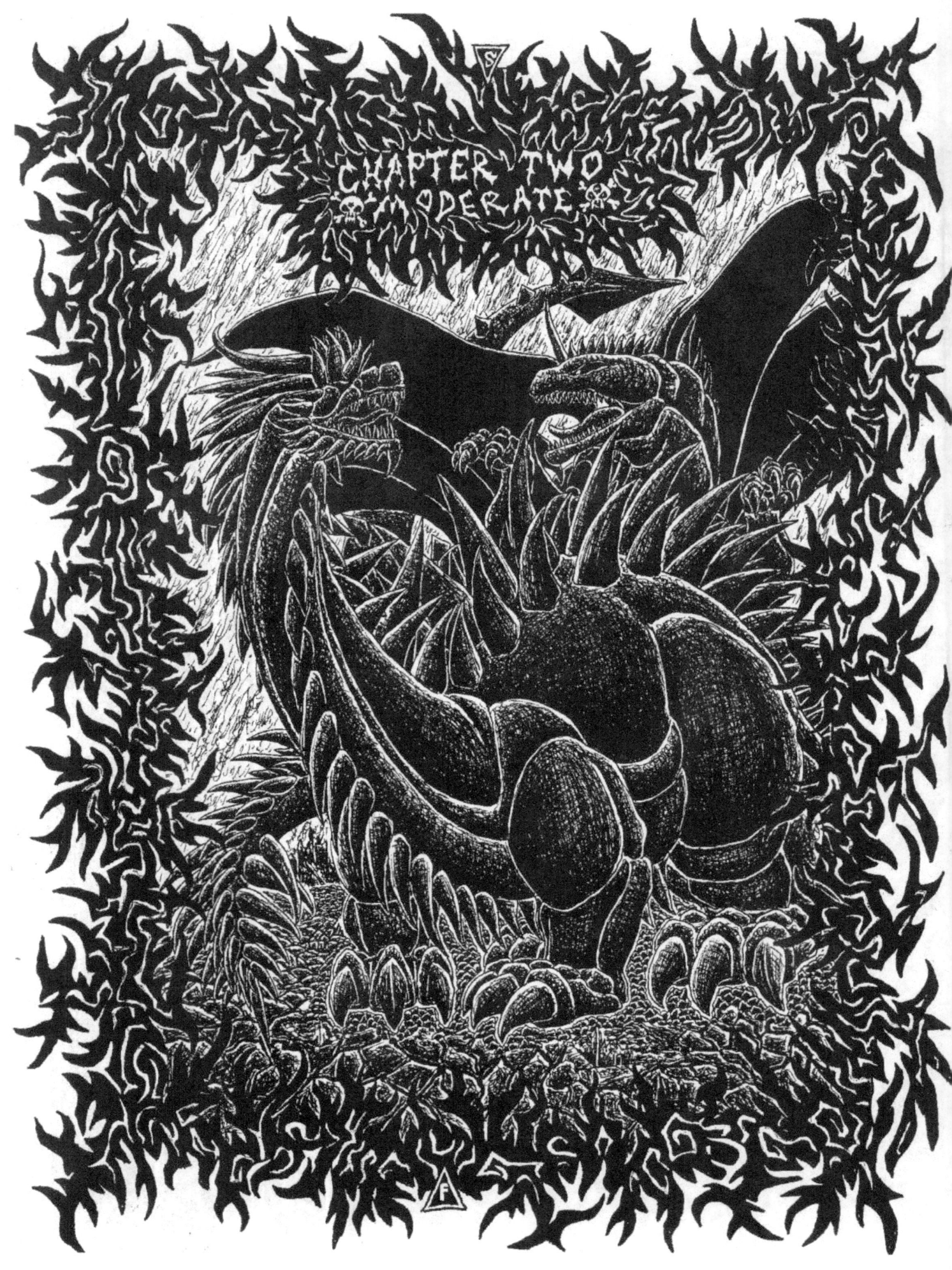

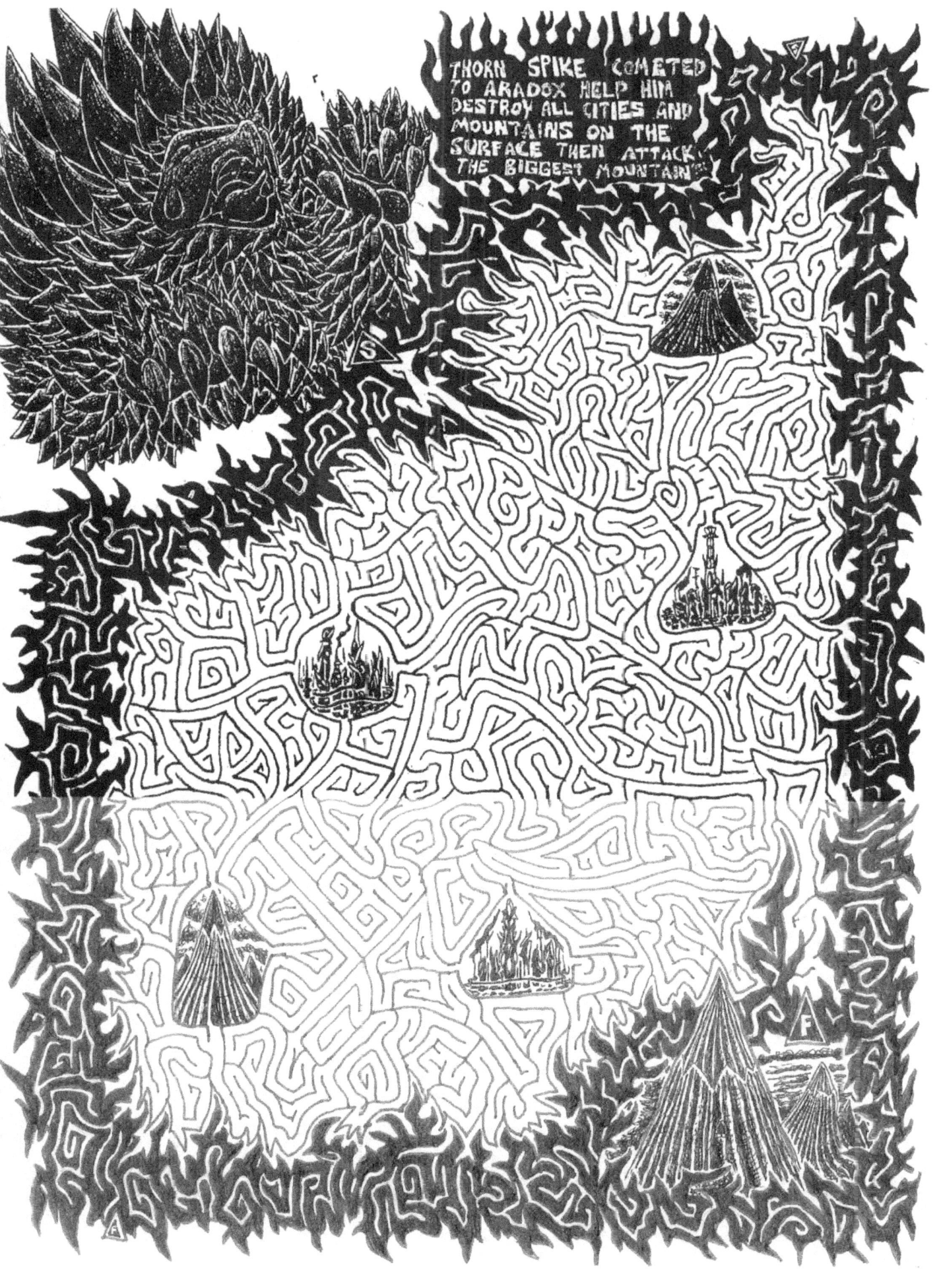

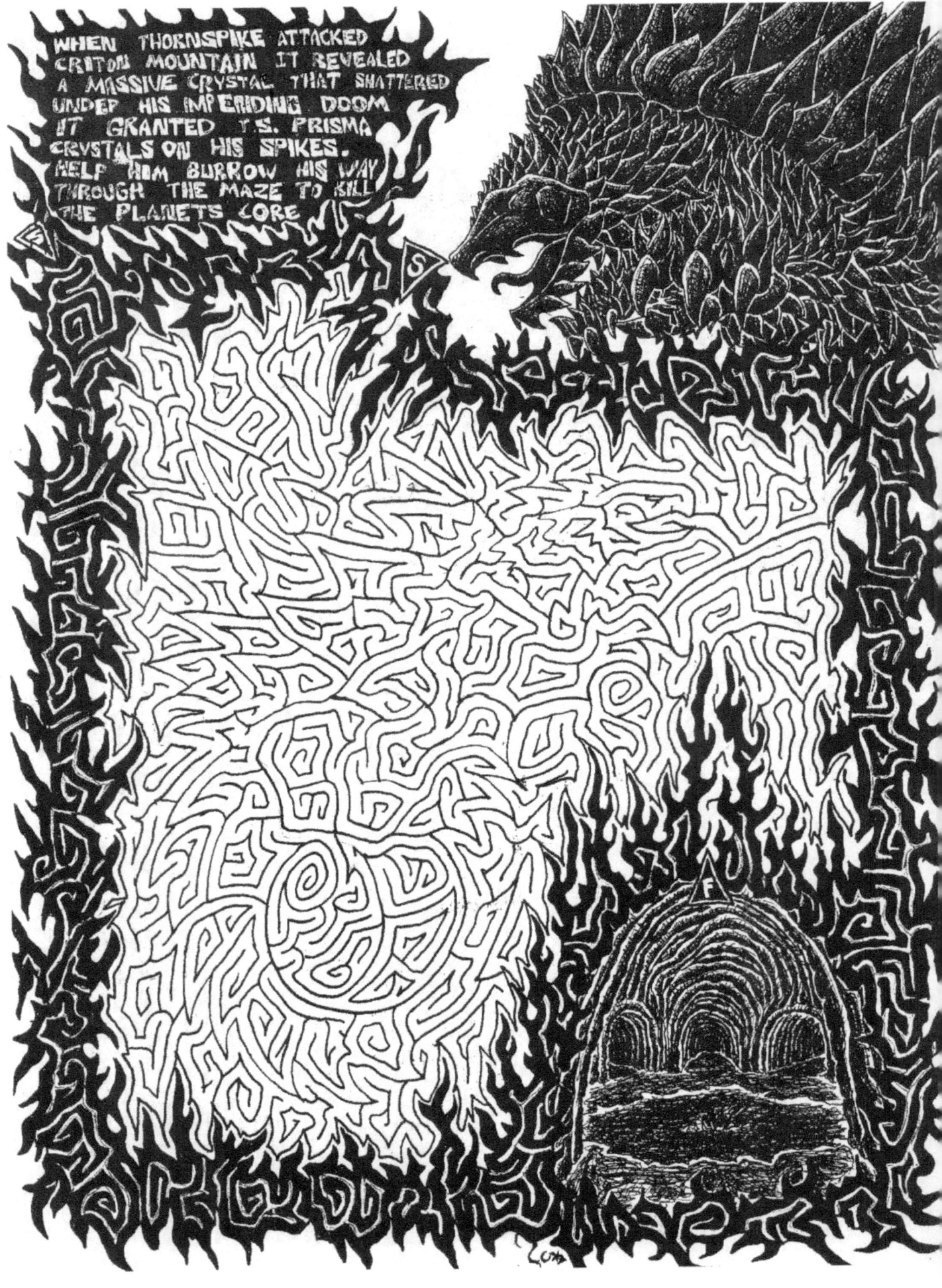

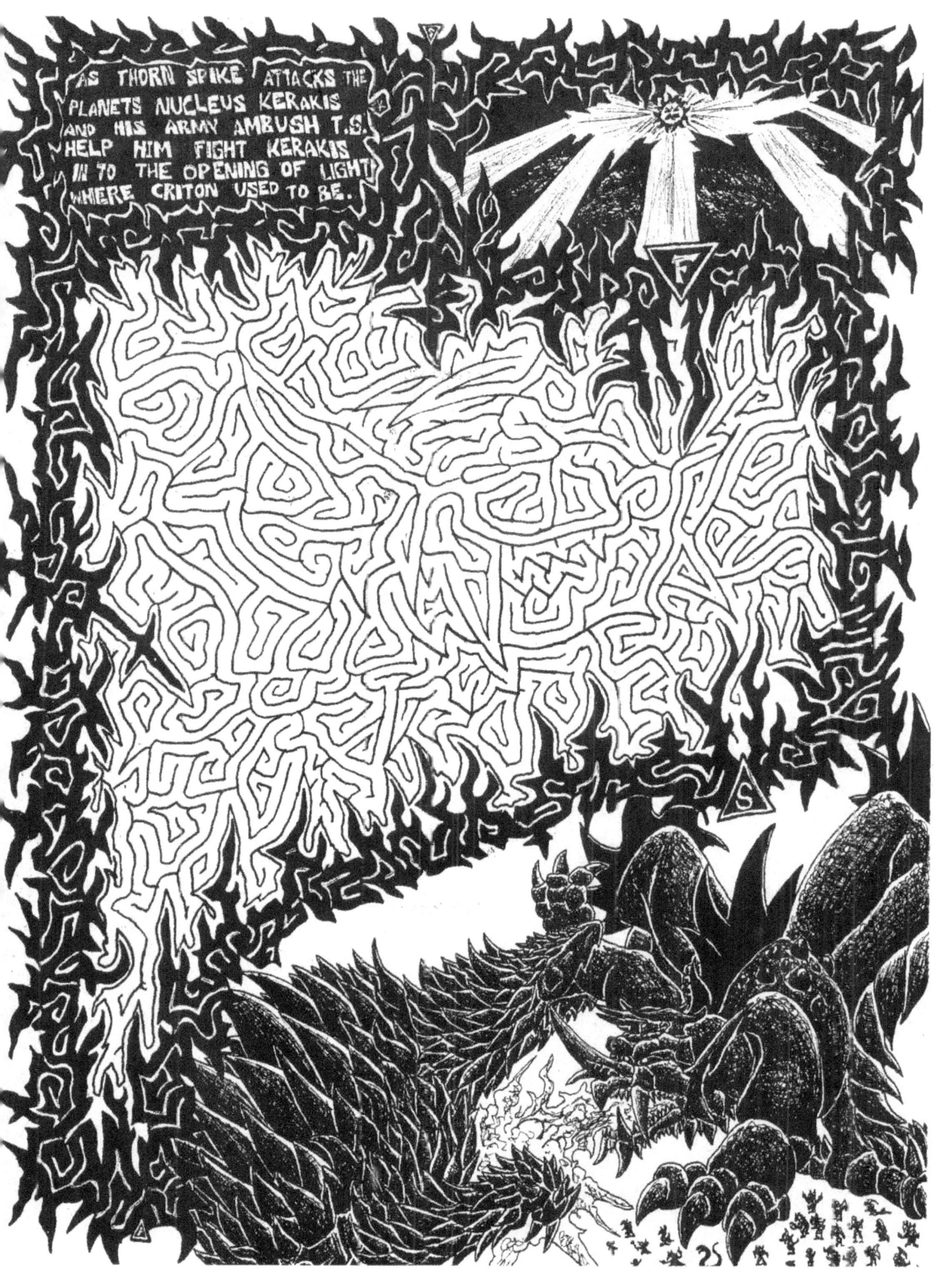

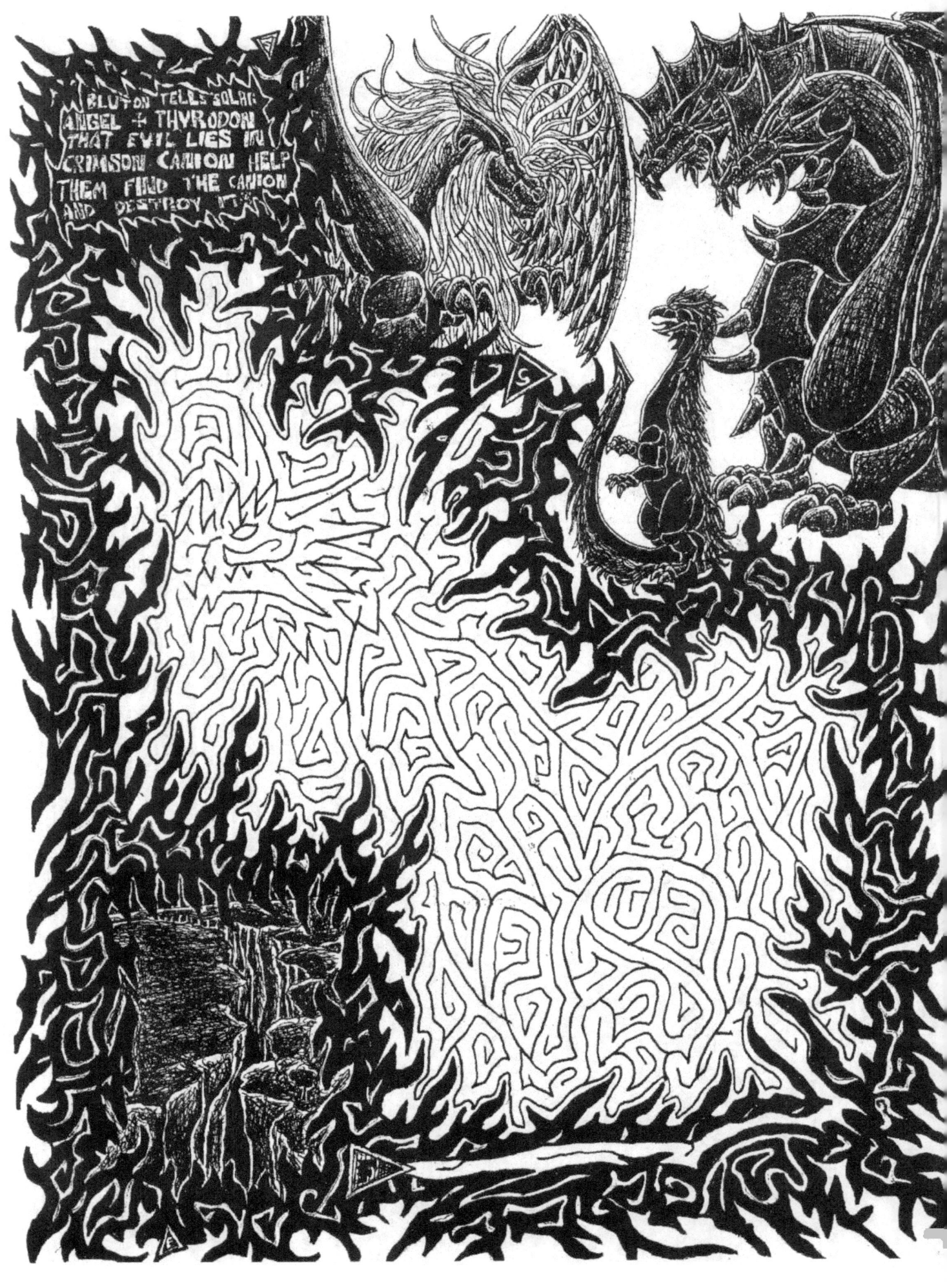

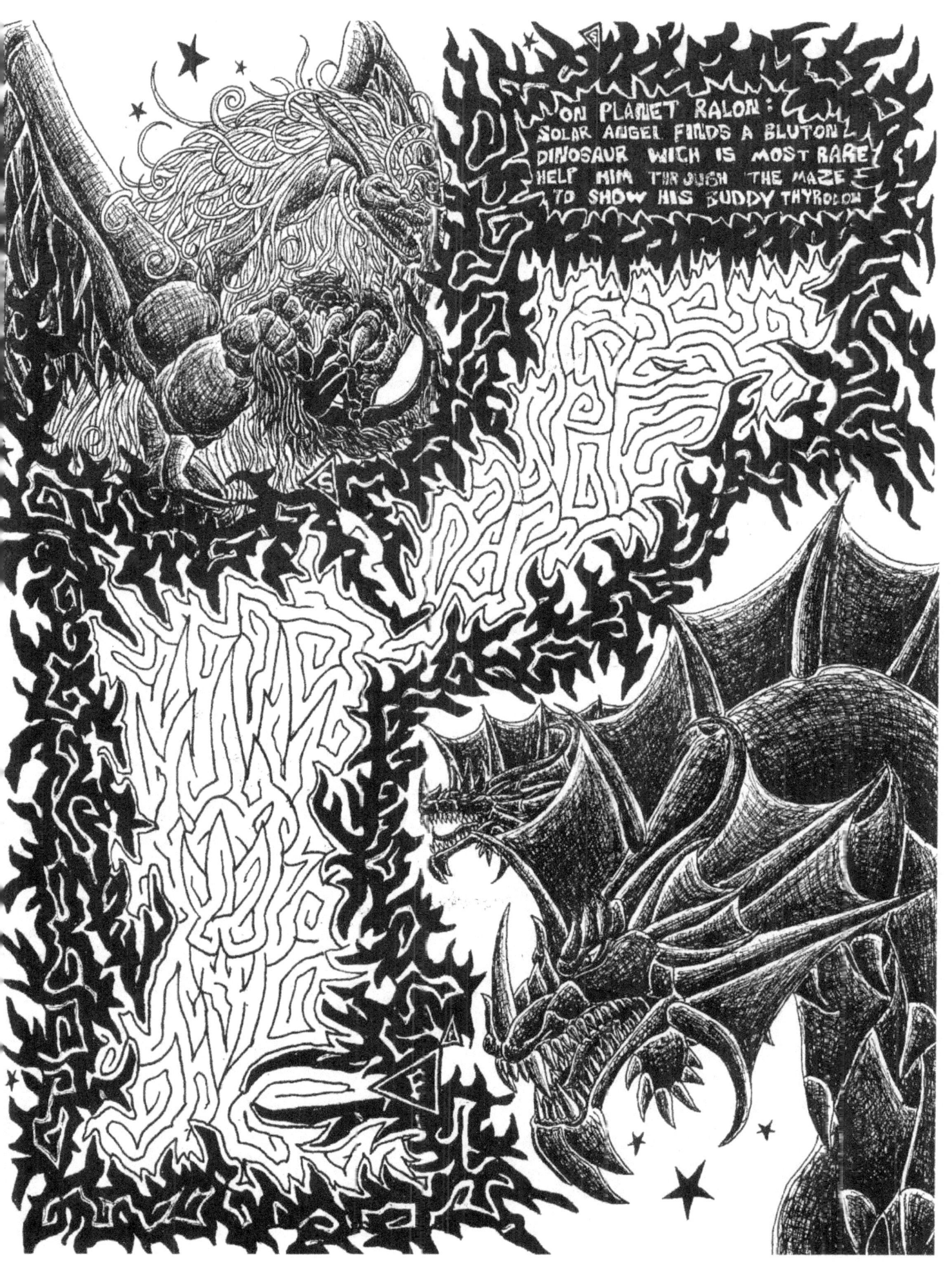

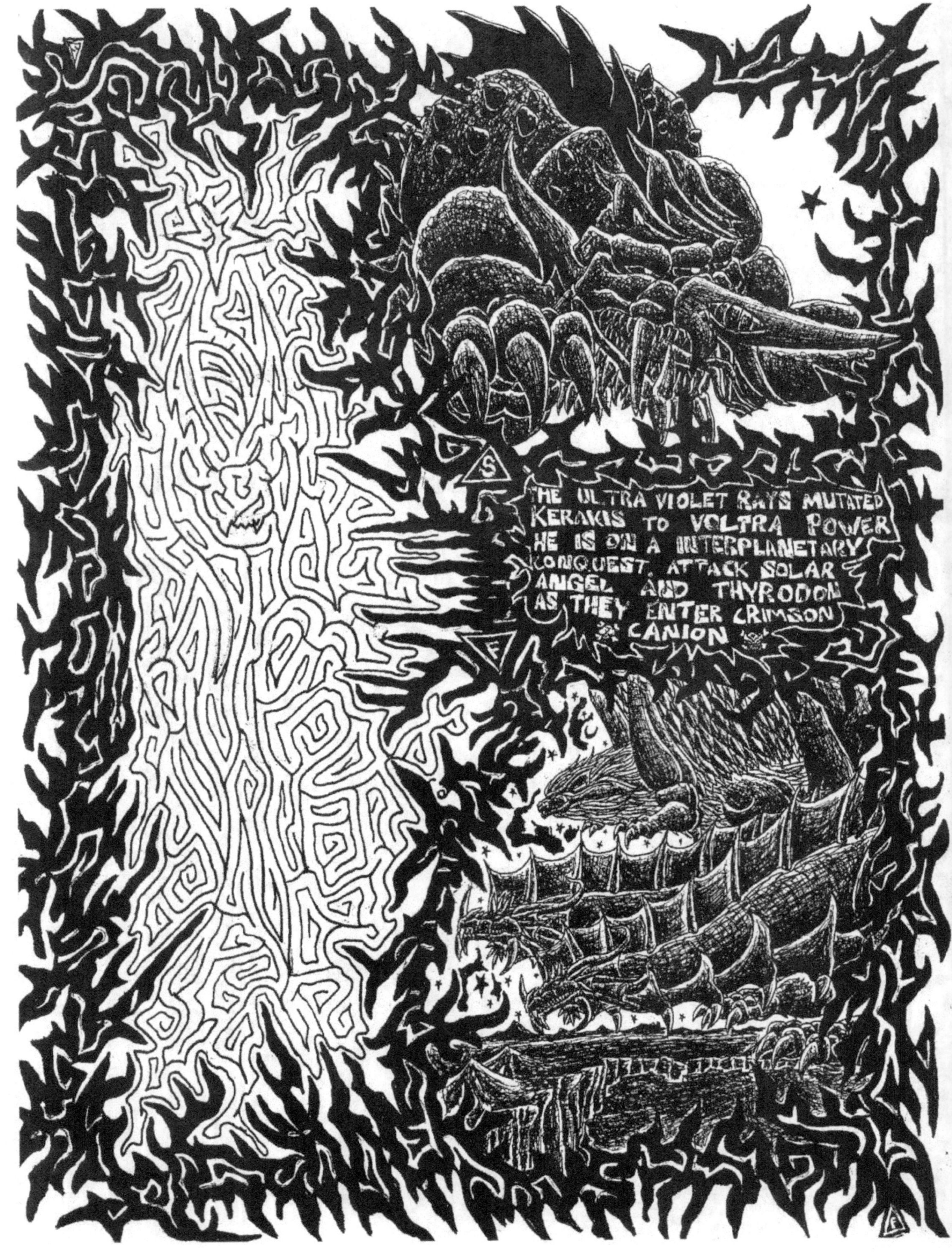

THE ULTRA VIOLET RAYS MUTATED KERAKIS TO VOLTRA POWER HE IS ON A INTERPLANETARY KONQUEST ATTACK SOLAR ANGEL AND THYRODON AS THEY ENTER CRIMSON CANION

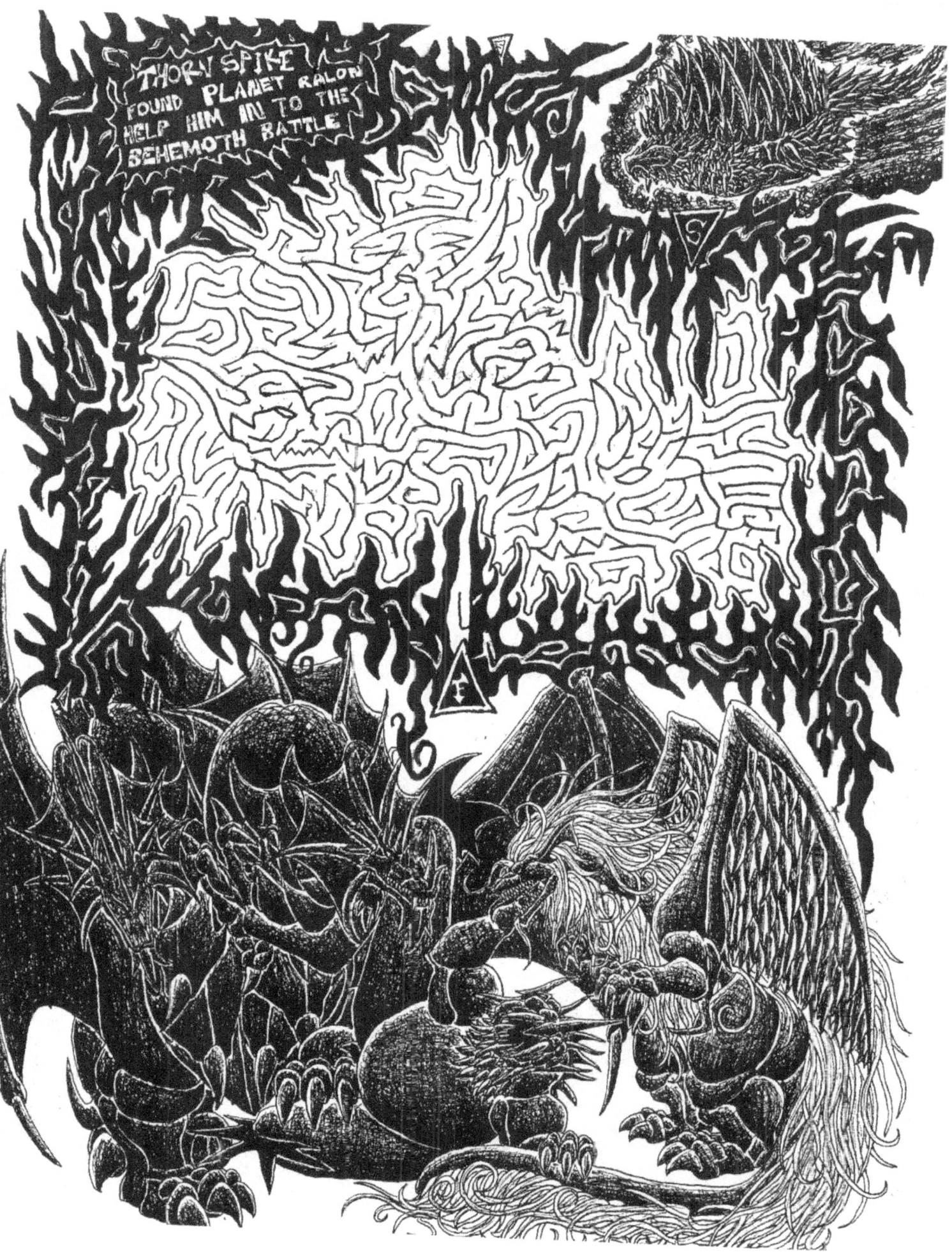

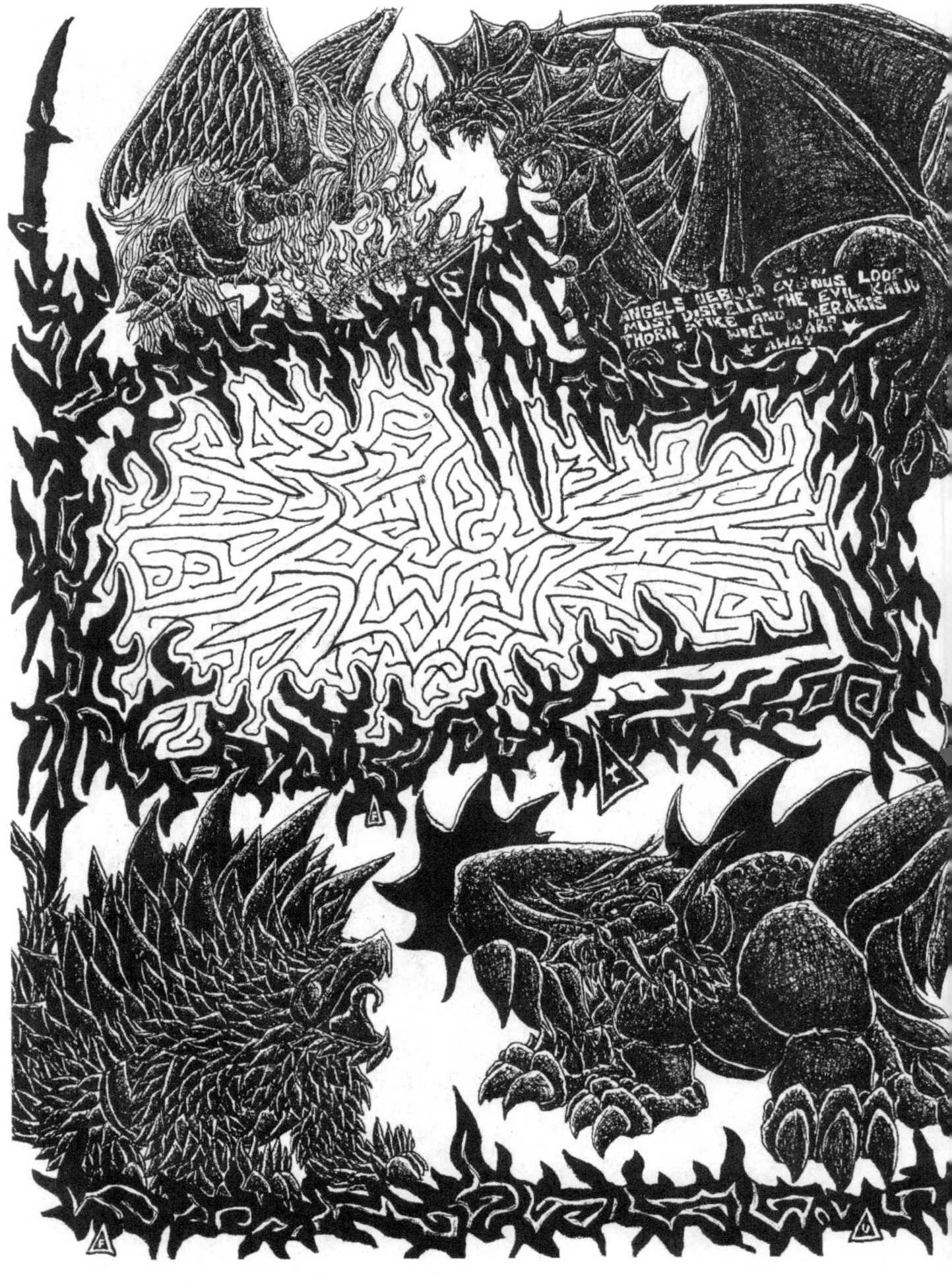

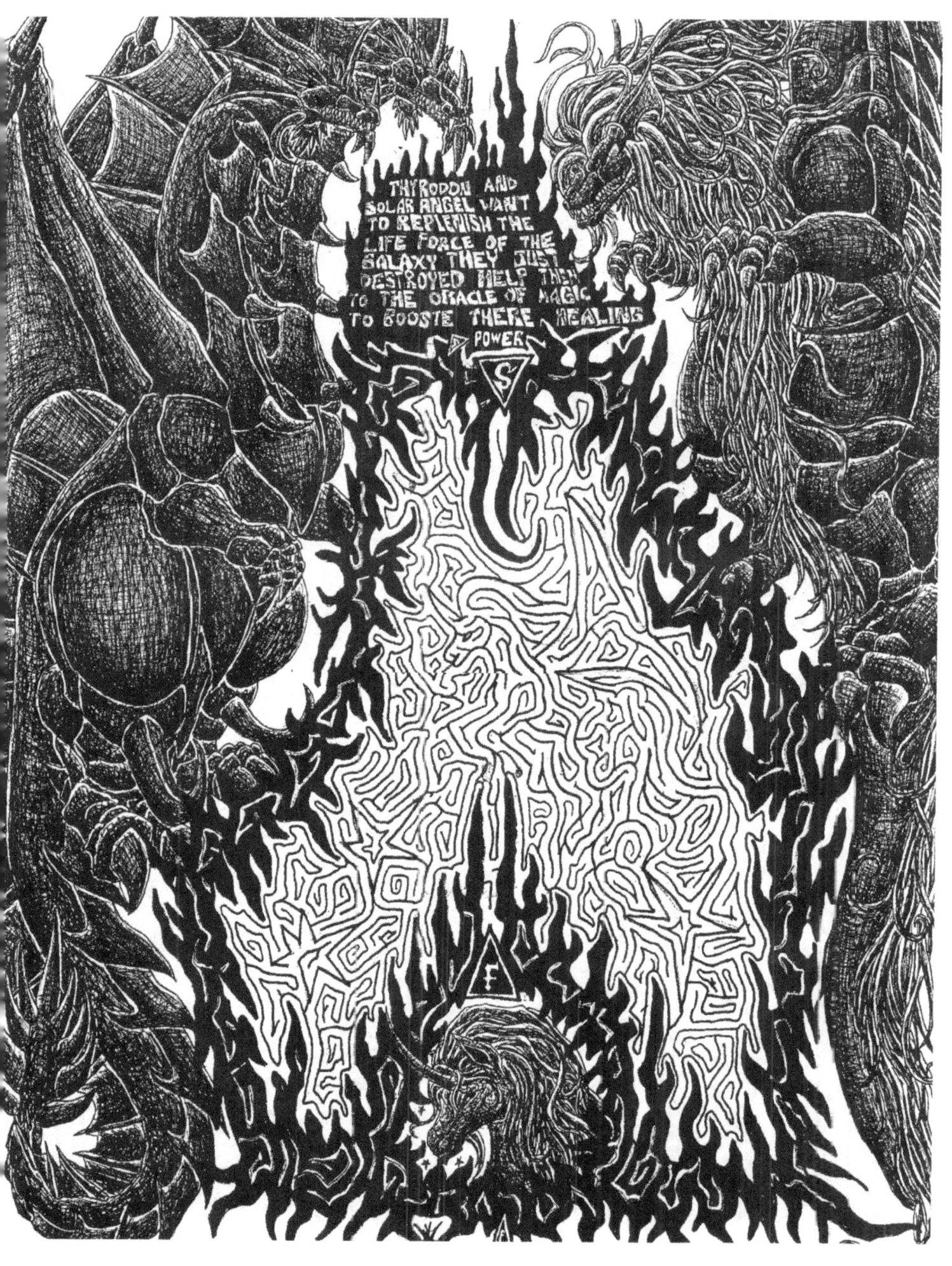

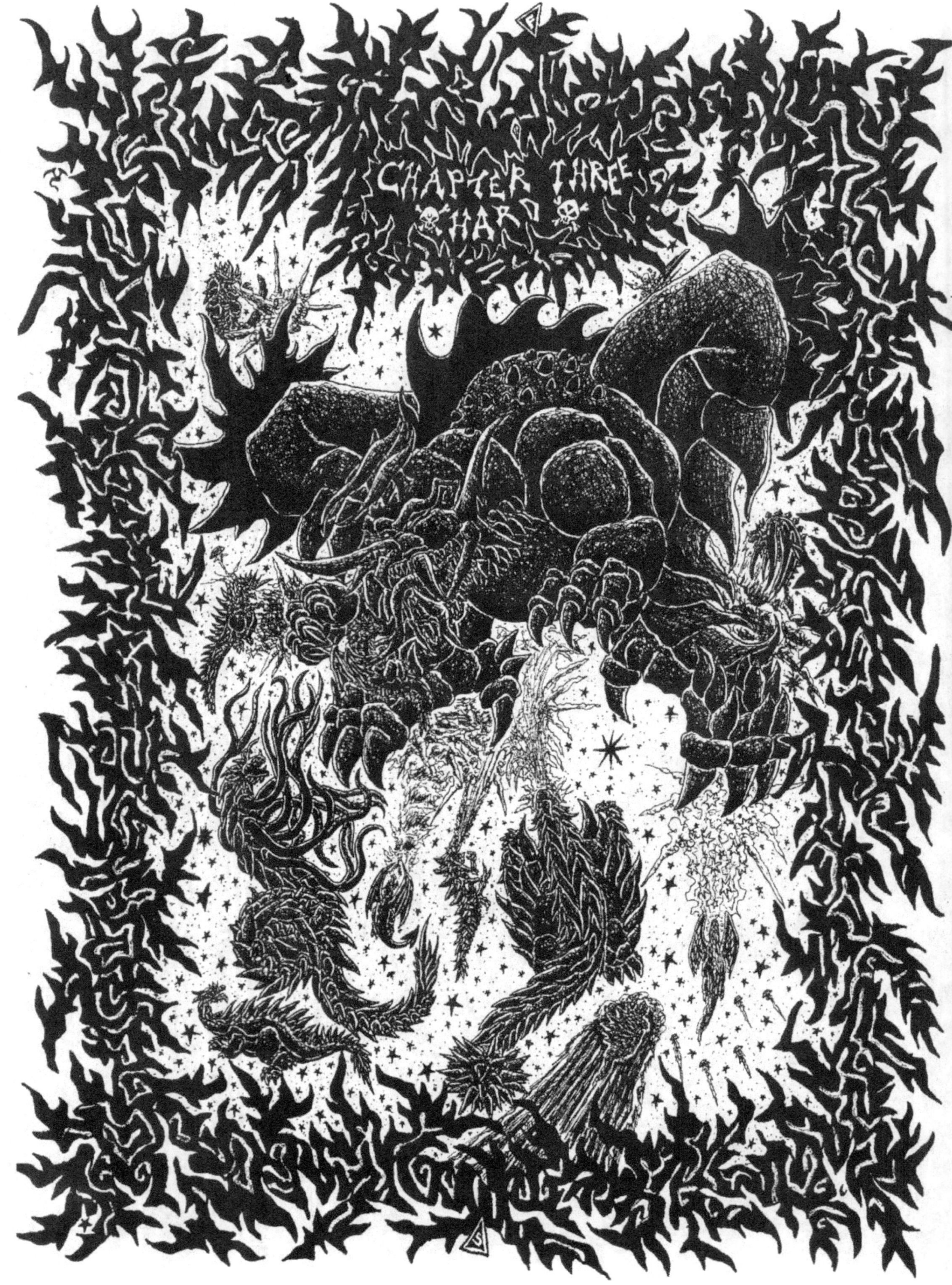

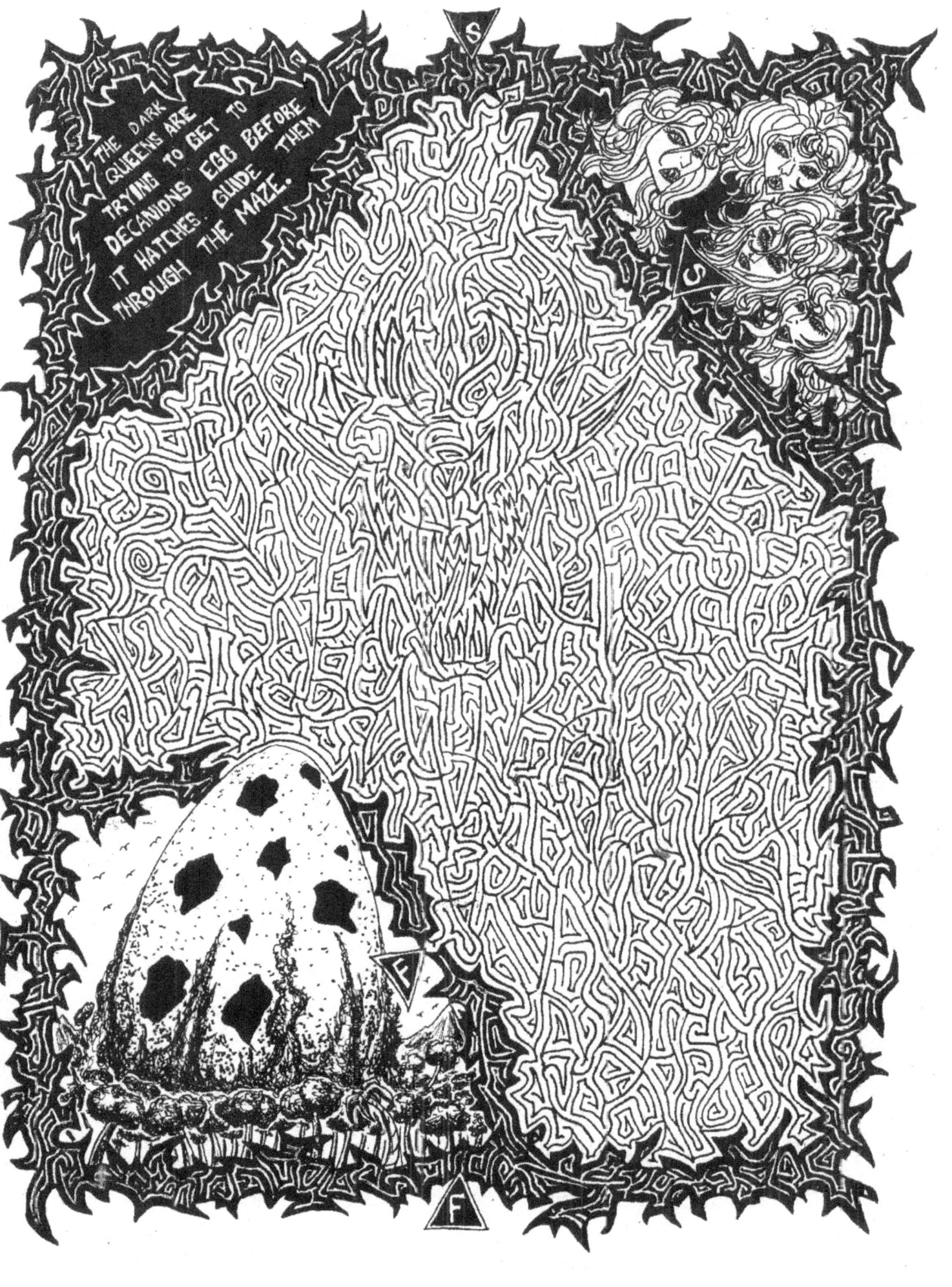

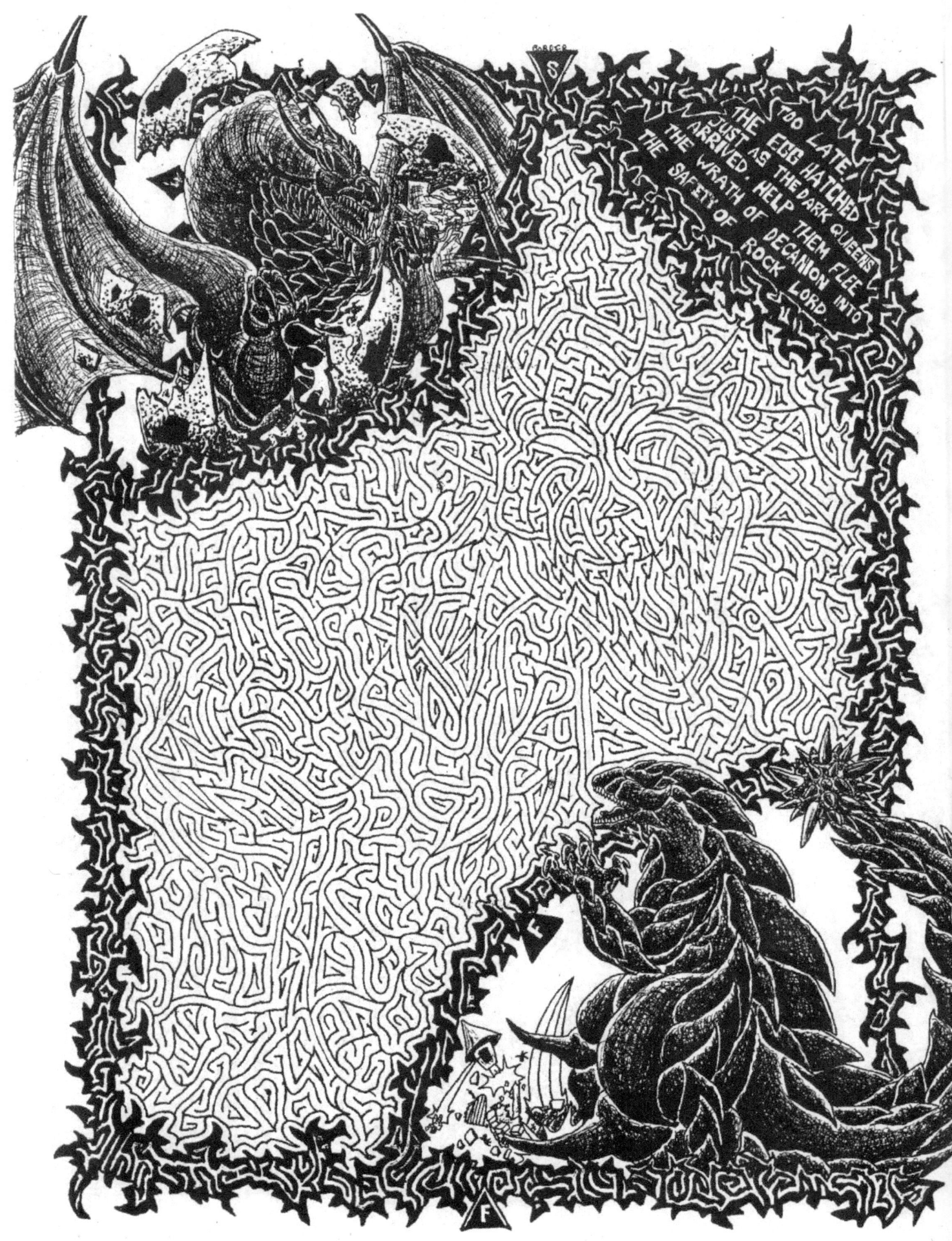

TOO LATE! THE EGG HATCHED JUST AS THE DARK QUEENS ARRIVED. HELP THEM FLEE THE WRATH OF DECAMON INTO THE SAFETY OF ROCK LORD

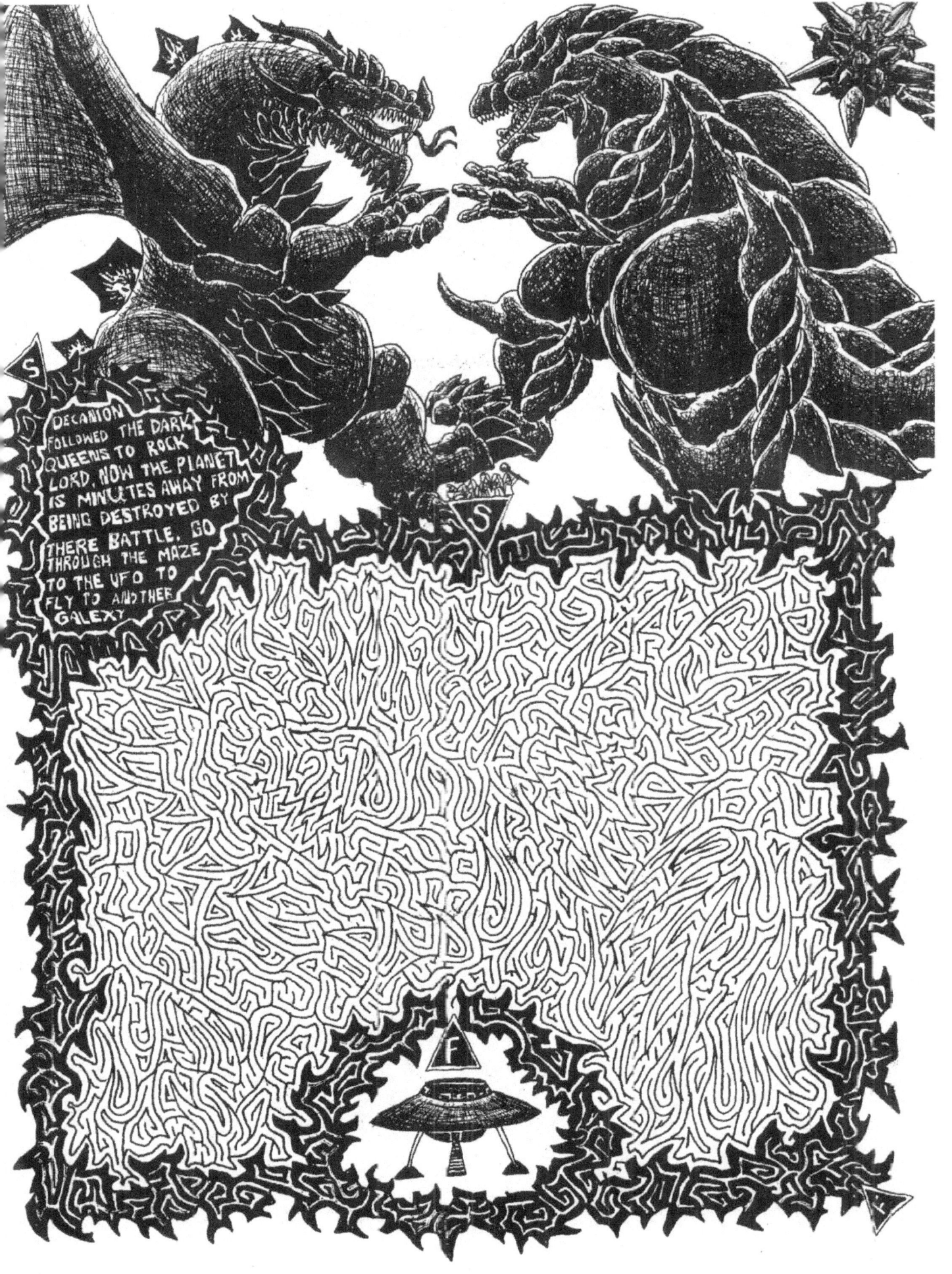

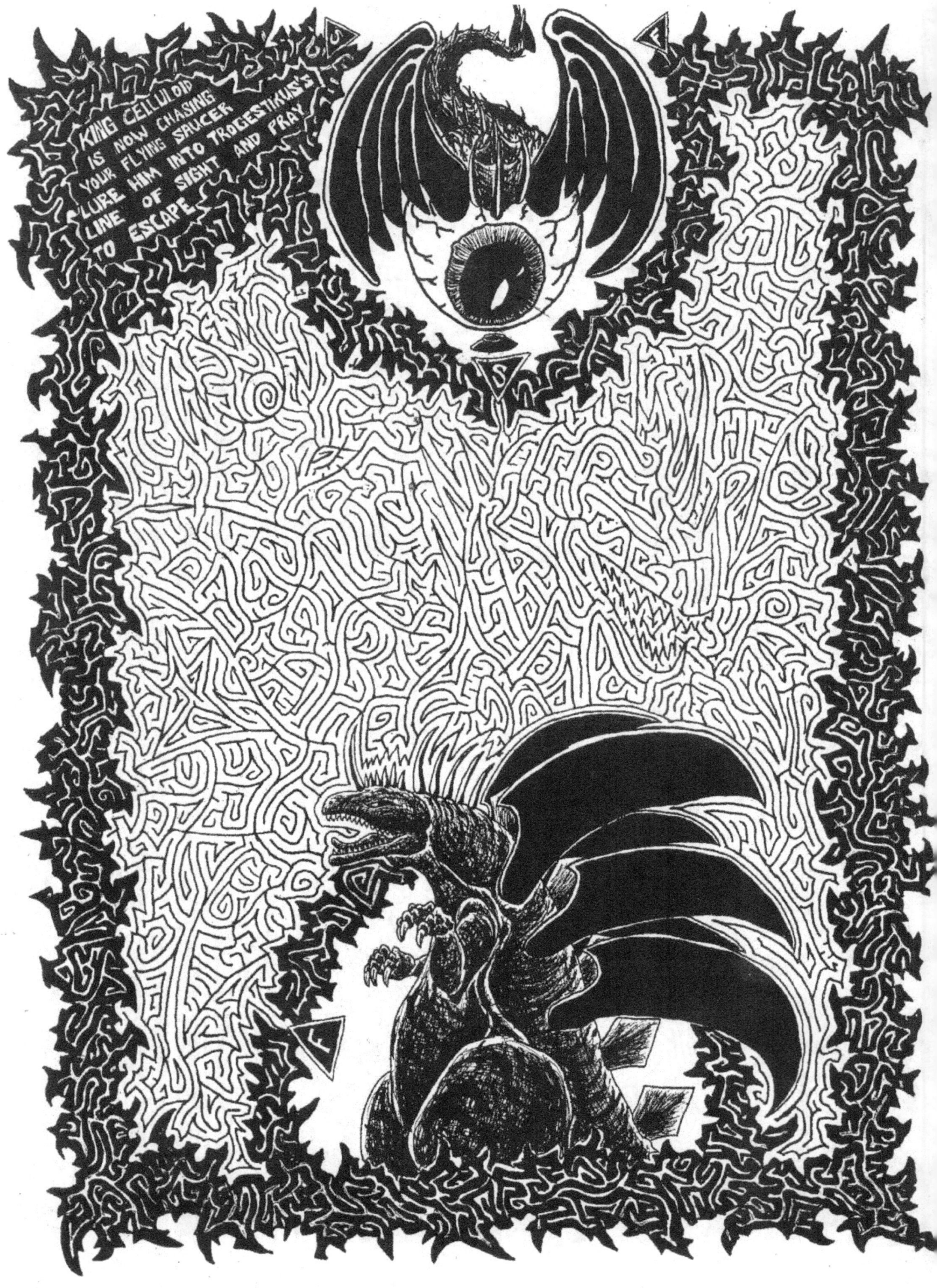

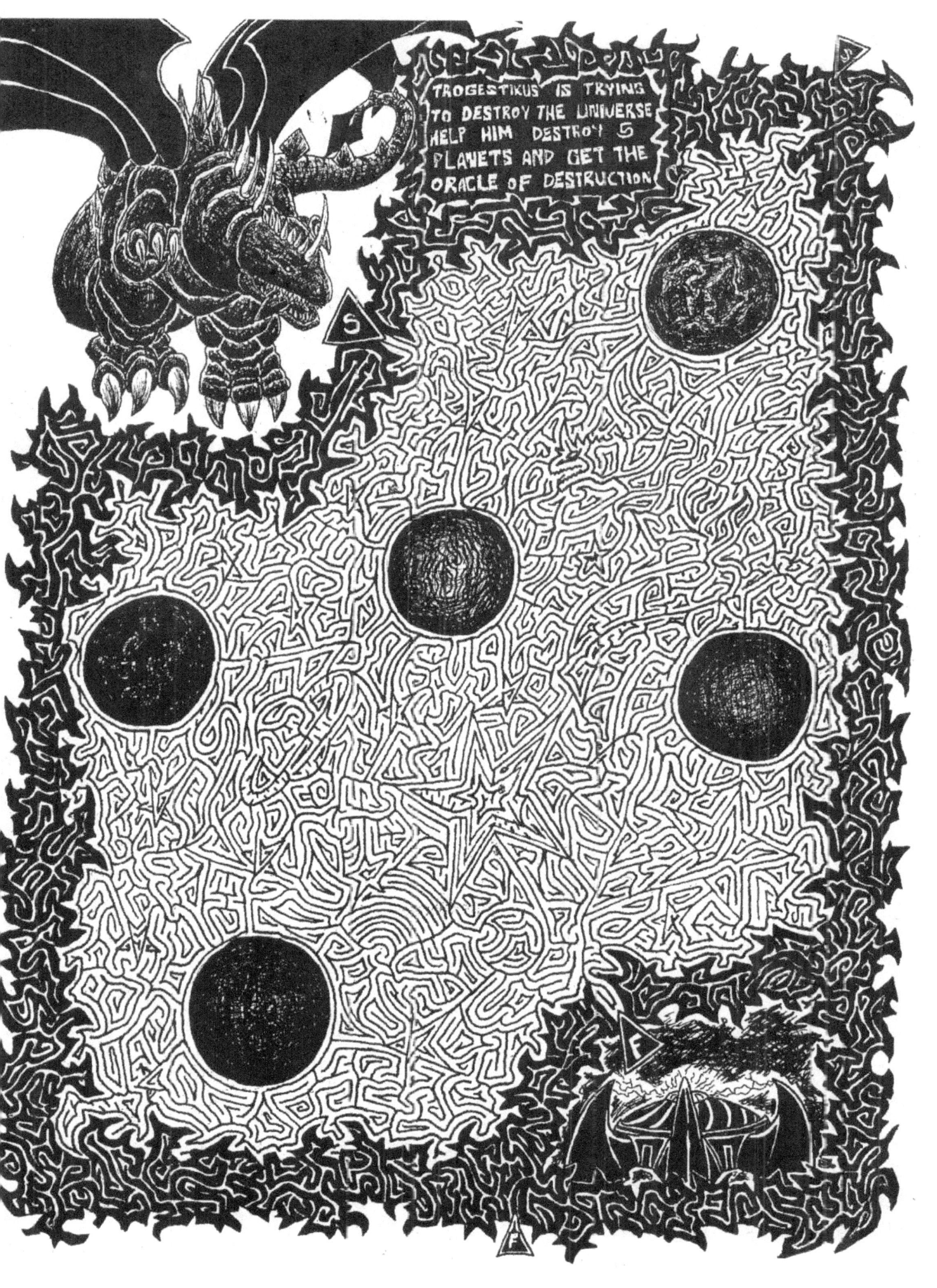

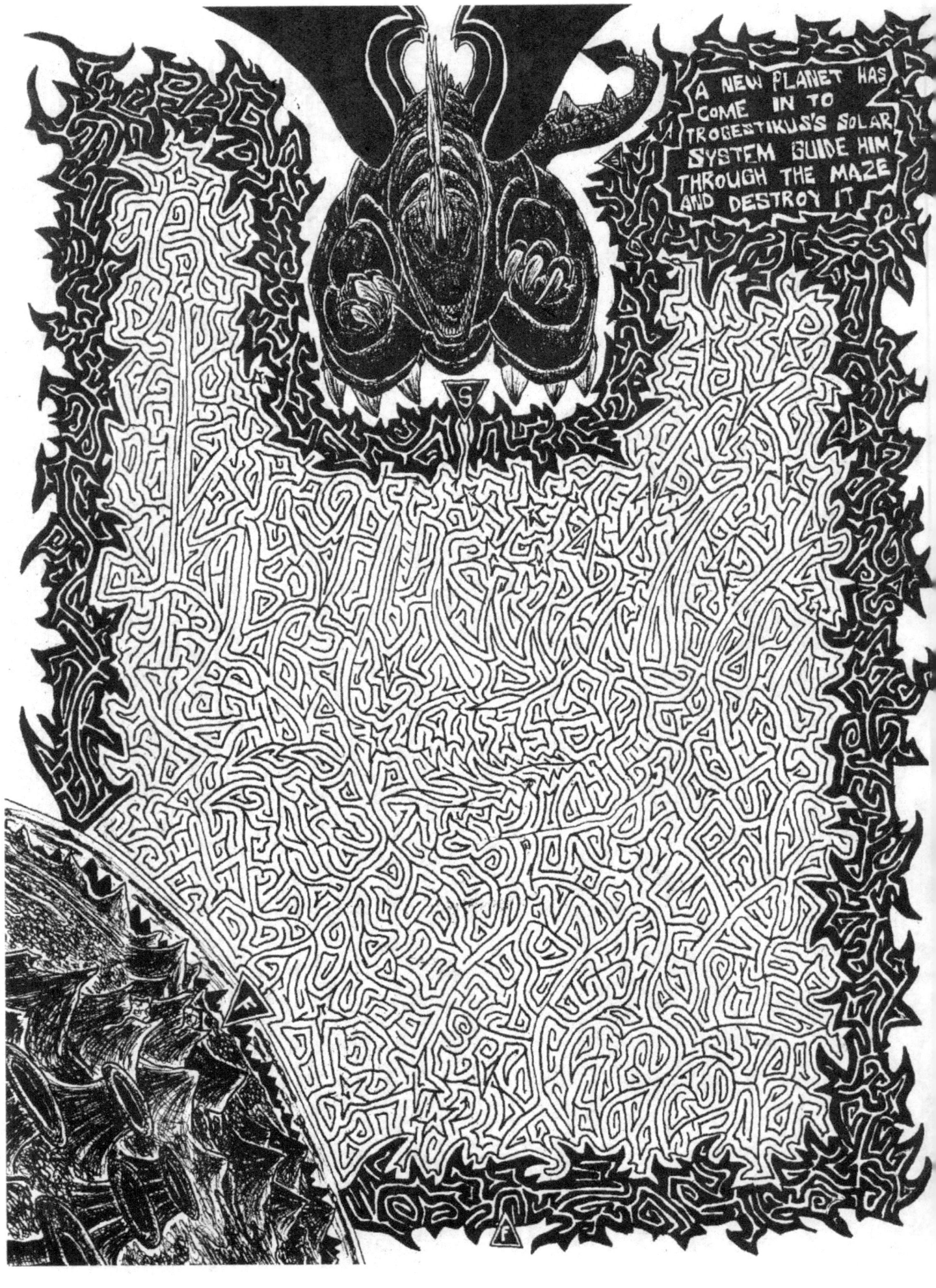

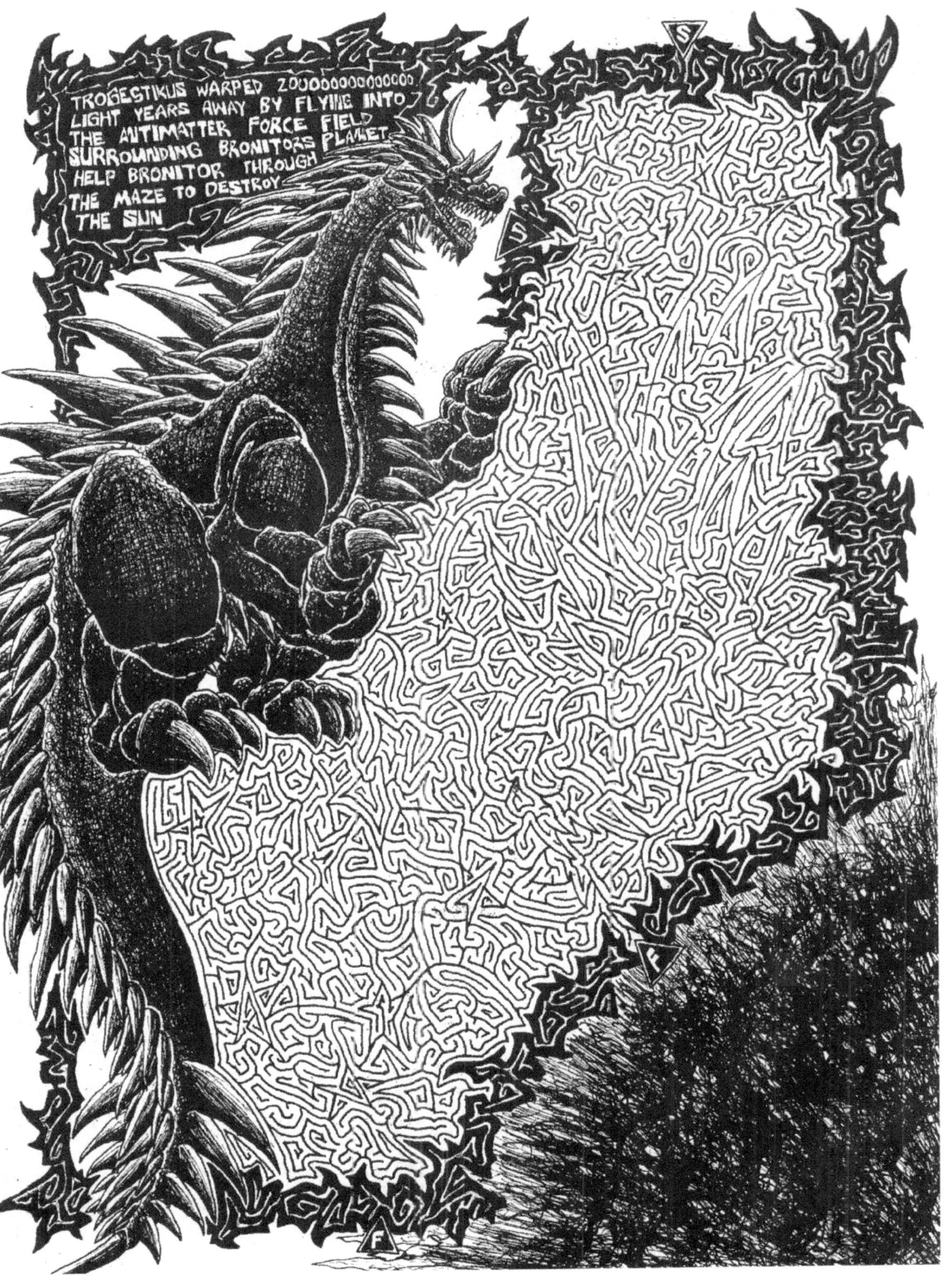

TROBESTIKUS WARPED ZOJOOOOOOOOOOO LIGHT YEARS AWAY BY FLYING INTO THE ANTIMATTER FORCE FIELD SURROUNDING BRONITORS PLANET HELP BRONITOR THROUGH THE MAZE TO DESTROY THE SUN

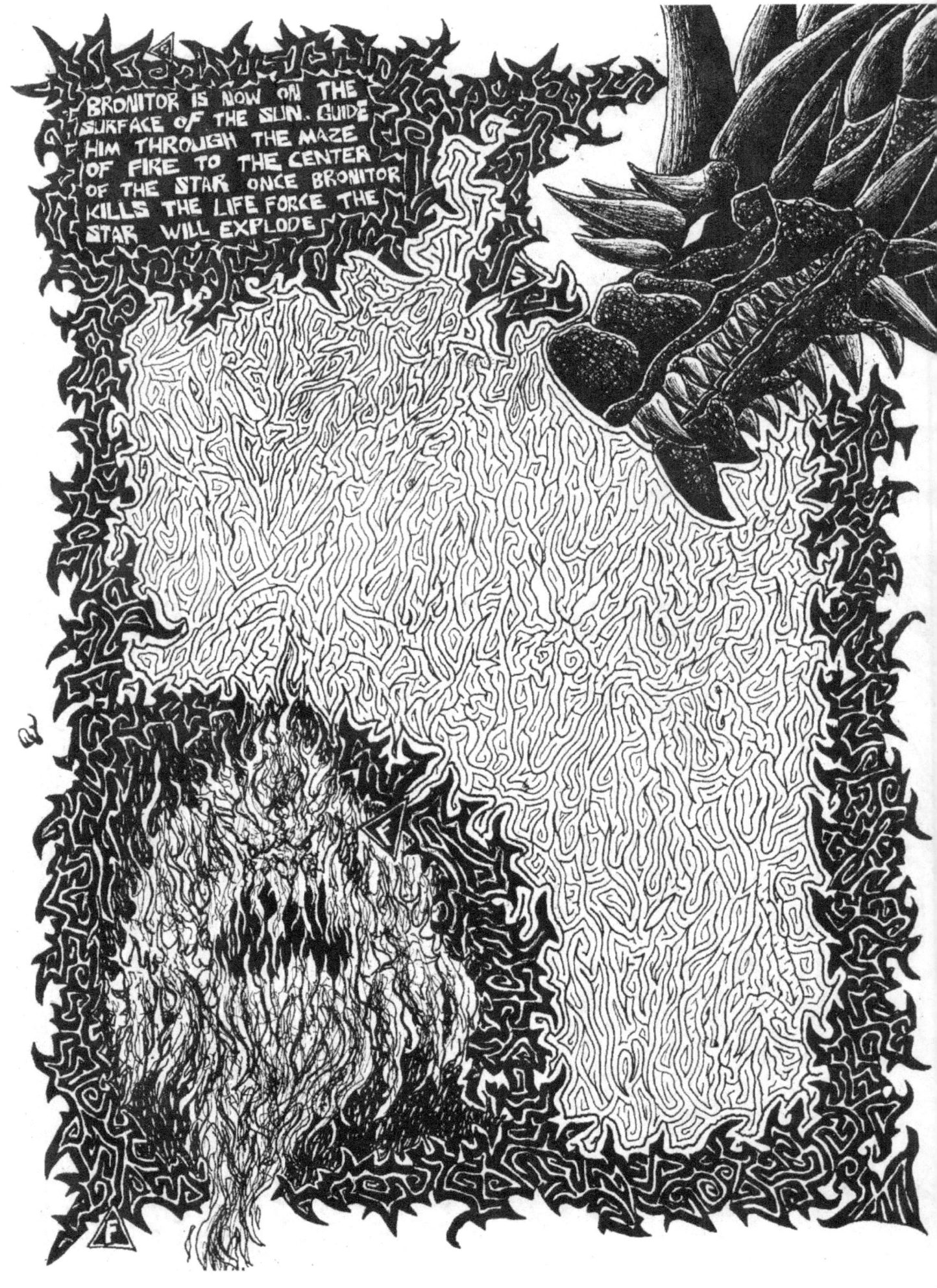

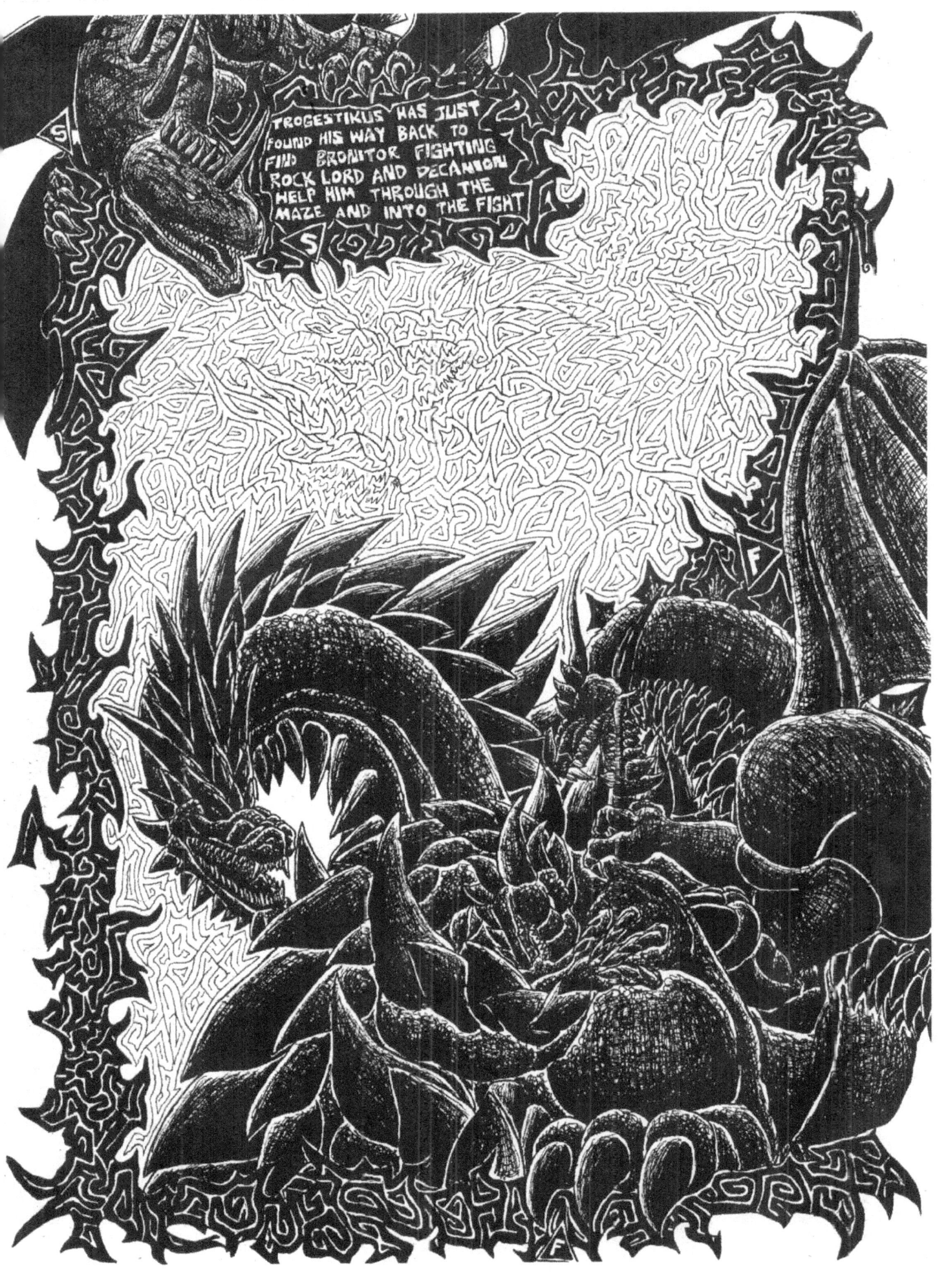

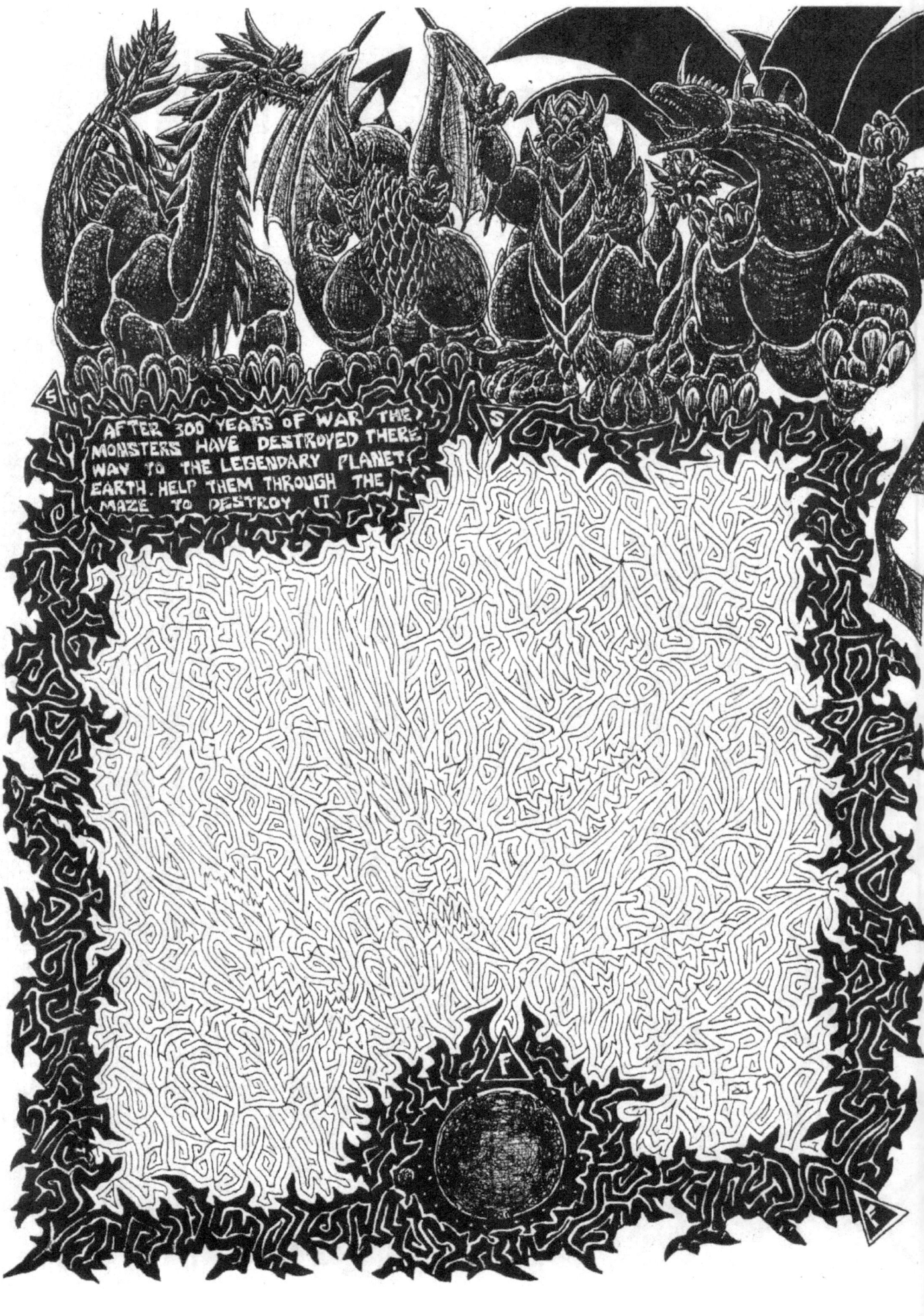

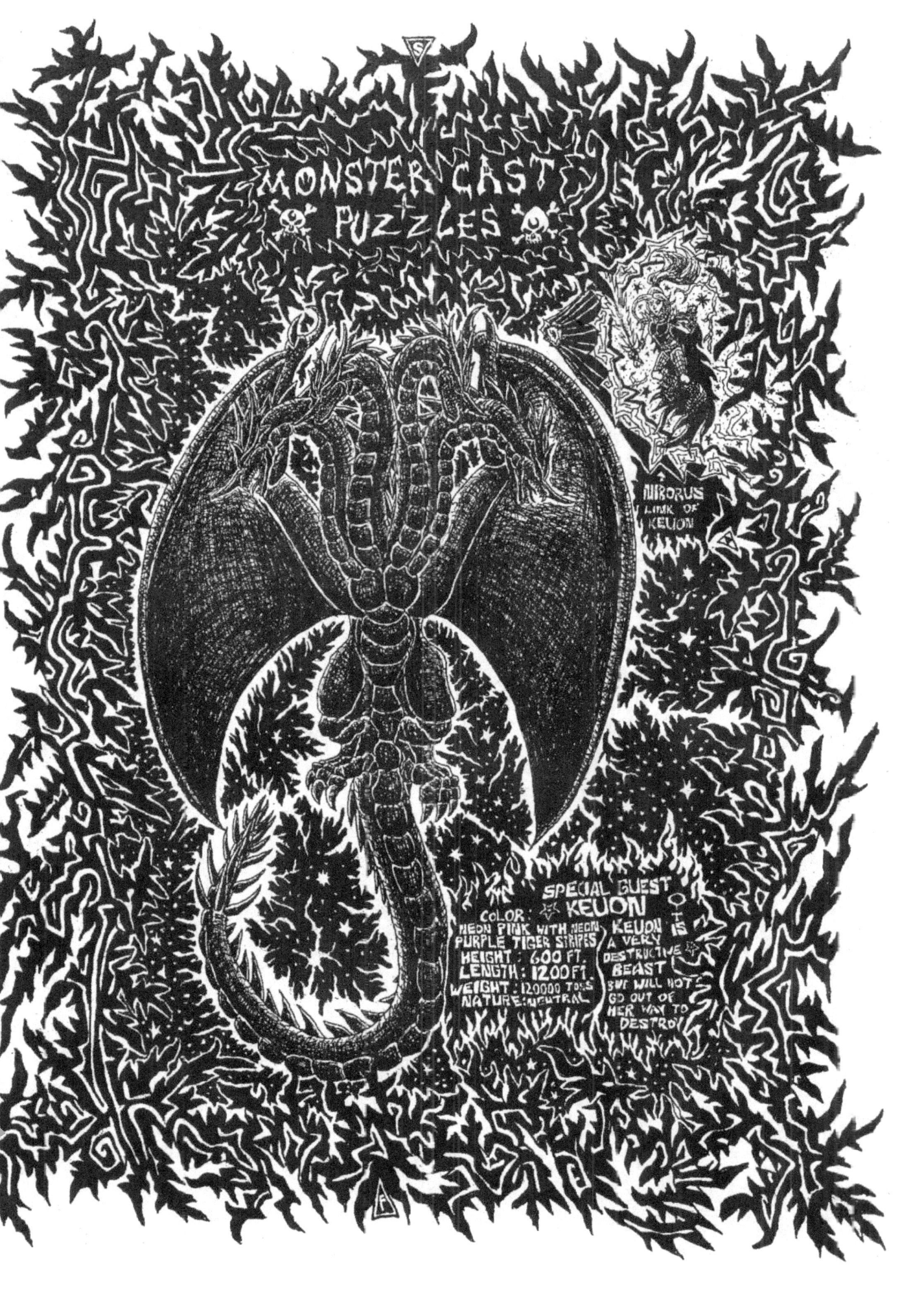

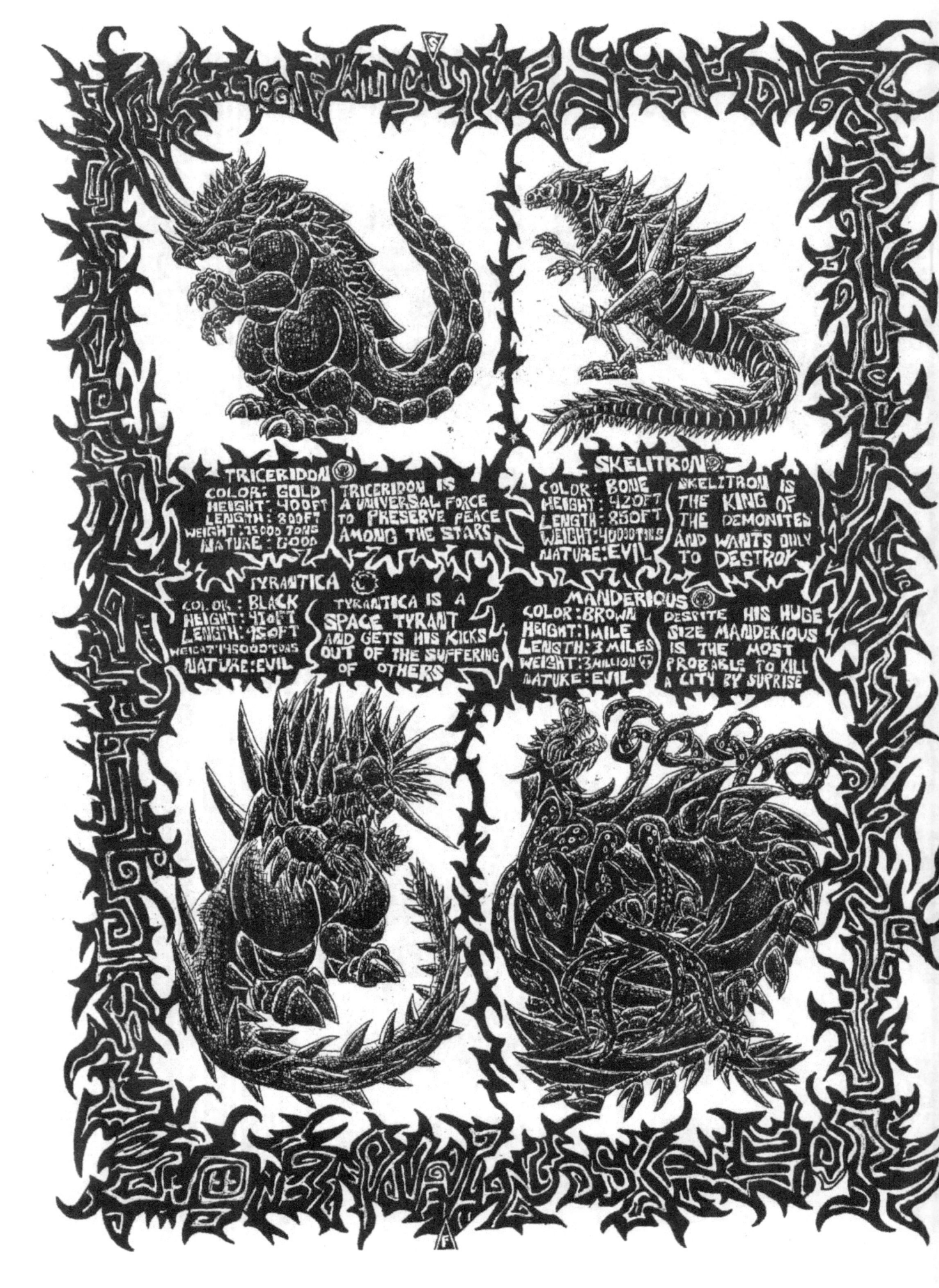

TRICERIDON
COLOR: GOLD
HEIGHT: 400FT
LENGTH: 800FT
WEIGHT: 15000 TONS
NATURE: GOOD

TRICERIDON IS A UNIVERSAL FORCE TO PRESERVE PEACE AMONG THE STARS

SKELITRON
COLOR: BONE
HEIGHT: 420FT
LENGTH: 850FT
WEIGHT: 40000 TONS
NATURE: EVIL

SKELITRON IS THE KING OF THE DEMONITES AND WANTS ONLY TO DESTROY

TYRANTICA
COLOR: BLACK
HEIGHT: 410FT
LENGTH: 950FT
WEIGHT: 45000 TONS
NATURE: EVIL

TYRANTICA IS A SPACE TYRANT AND GETS HIS KICKS OUT OF THE SUFFERING OF OTHERS

MANDERIOUS
COLOR: BROWN
HEIGHT: 1 MILE
LENGTH: 3 MILES
WEIGHT: 3 MILLION T
NATURE: EVIL

DESPITE HIS HUGE SIZE MANDERIOUS IS THE MOST PROBABLE TO KILL A CITY BY SUPRISE

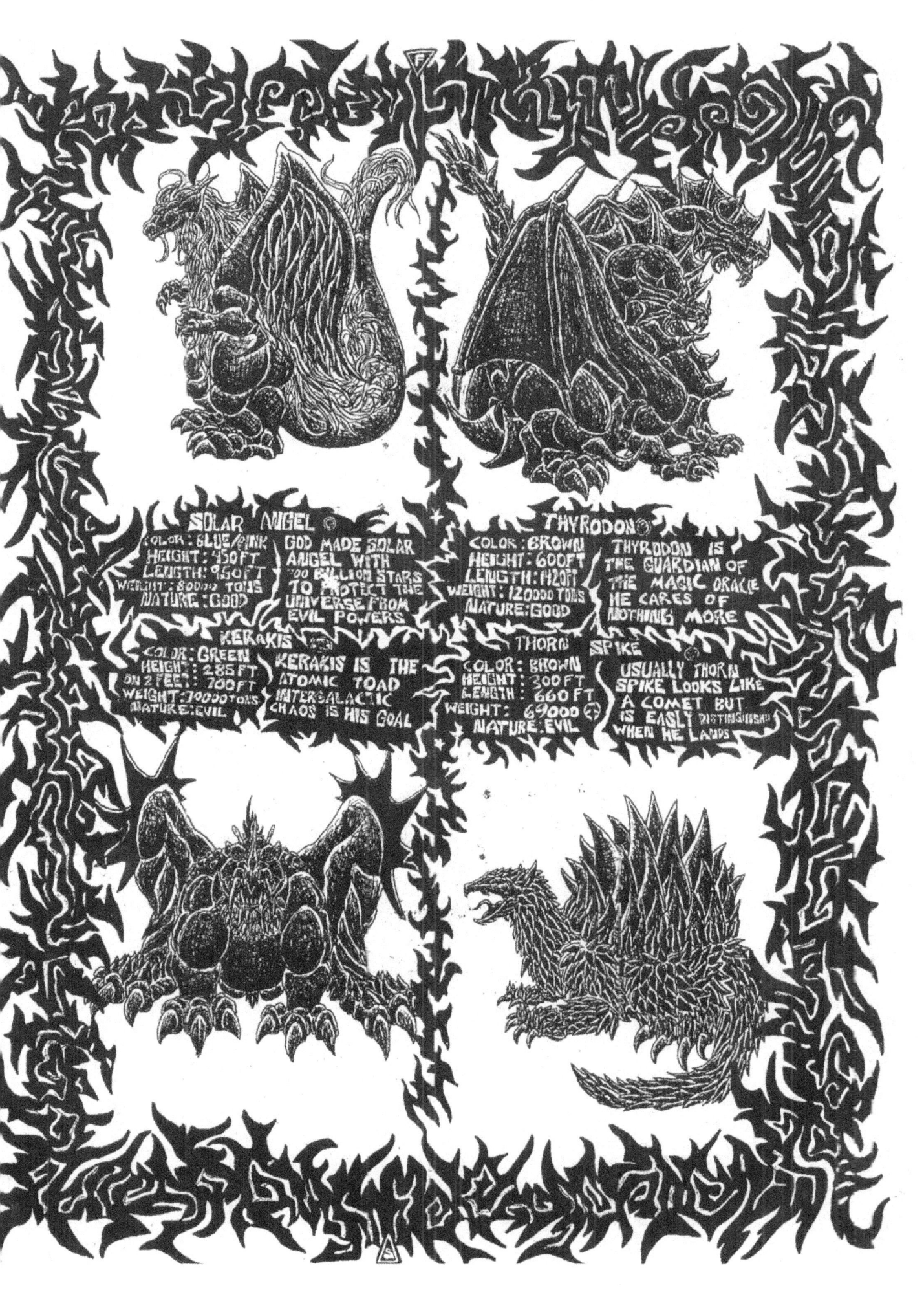

SOLAR ANGEL
COLOR: BLUE/PINK
HEIGHT: 450FT
LENGTH: 950FT
WEIGHT: 80000 TONS
NATURE: GOOD

GOD MADE SOLAR ANGEL WITH 700 BILLION STARS TO PROTECT THE UNIVERSE FROM EVIL POWERS

KERAKIS
COLOR: GREEN
HEIGHT: 285 FT
ON 2 FEET: 700FT
WEIGHT: 70000 TONS
NATURE: EVIL

KERAKIS IS THE ATOMIC TOAD INTERGALACTIC CHAOS IS HIS GOAL

THYRODON
COLOR: BROWN
HEIGHT: 600FT
LENGTH: 1420FT
WEIGHT: 120000 TONS
NATURE: GOOD

THYRODON IS THE GUARDIAN OF THE MAGIC ORACLE HE CARES OF NOTHING MORE

THORN SPIKE
COLOR: BROWN
HEIGHT: 300FT
LENGTH: 660 FT
WEIGHT: 69000
NATURE: EVIL

USUALLY THORN SPIKE LOOKS LIKE A COMET BUT IS EASLY DISTINGUISHED WHEN HE LANDS

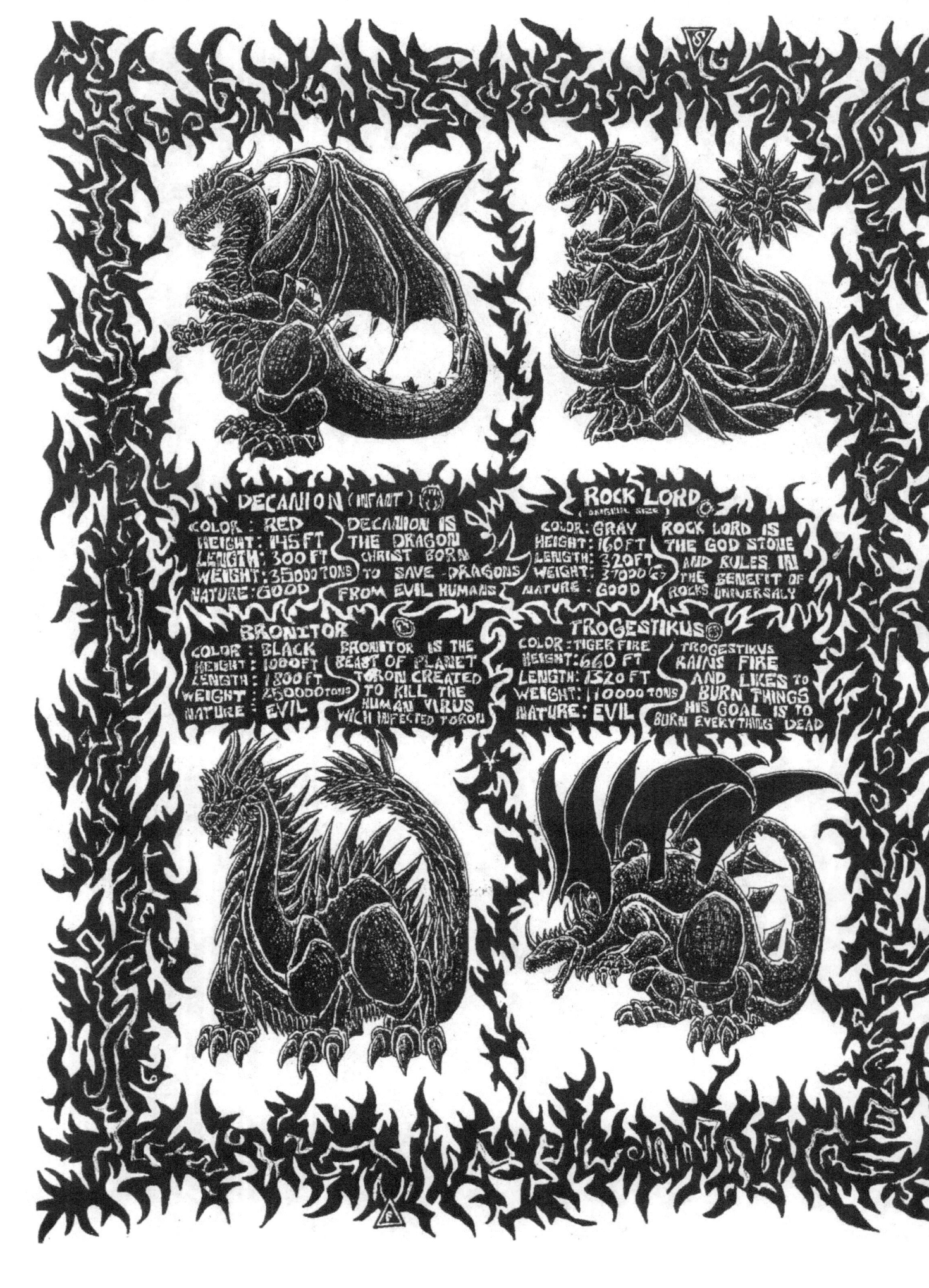

DECANION (INFANT)

COLOR: RED
HEIGHT: 145 FT
LENGTH: 300 FT
WEIGHT: 35000 TONS
NATURE: GOOD

DECANION IS THE DRAGON CHRIST BORN TO SAVE DRAGONS FROM EVIL HUMANS

ROCK LORD

COLOR: GRAY
HEIGHT: 160 FT
LENGTH: 320 FT
WEIGHT: 37000 C7
NATURE: GOOD

ROCK LORD IS THE GOD STONE AND RULES IN THE BENEFIT OF ROCKS UNIVERSALY

BRONITOR

COLOR: BLACK
HEIGHT: 1080 FT
LENGTH: 1800 FT
WEIGHT: 250000 TONS
NATURE: EVIL

BRONITOR IS THE BEAST OF PLANET TORON CREATED TO KILL THE HUMAN VIRUS WICH INFECTED TORON

TROGESTIKUS

COLOR: TIGER FIRE
HEIGHT: 660 FT
LENGTH: 1320 FT
WEIGHT: 110000 TONS
NATURE: EVIL

TROGESTIKUS RAINS FIRE AND LIKES TO BURN THINGS HIS GOAL IS TO BURN EVERYTHING DEAD

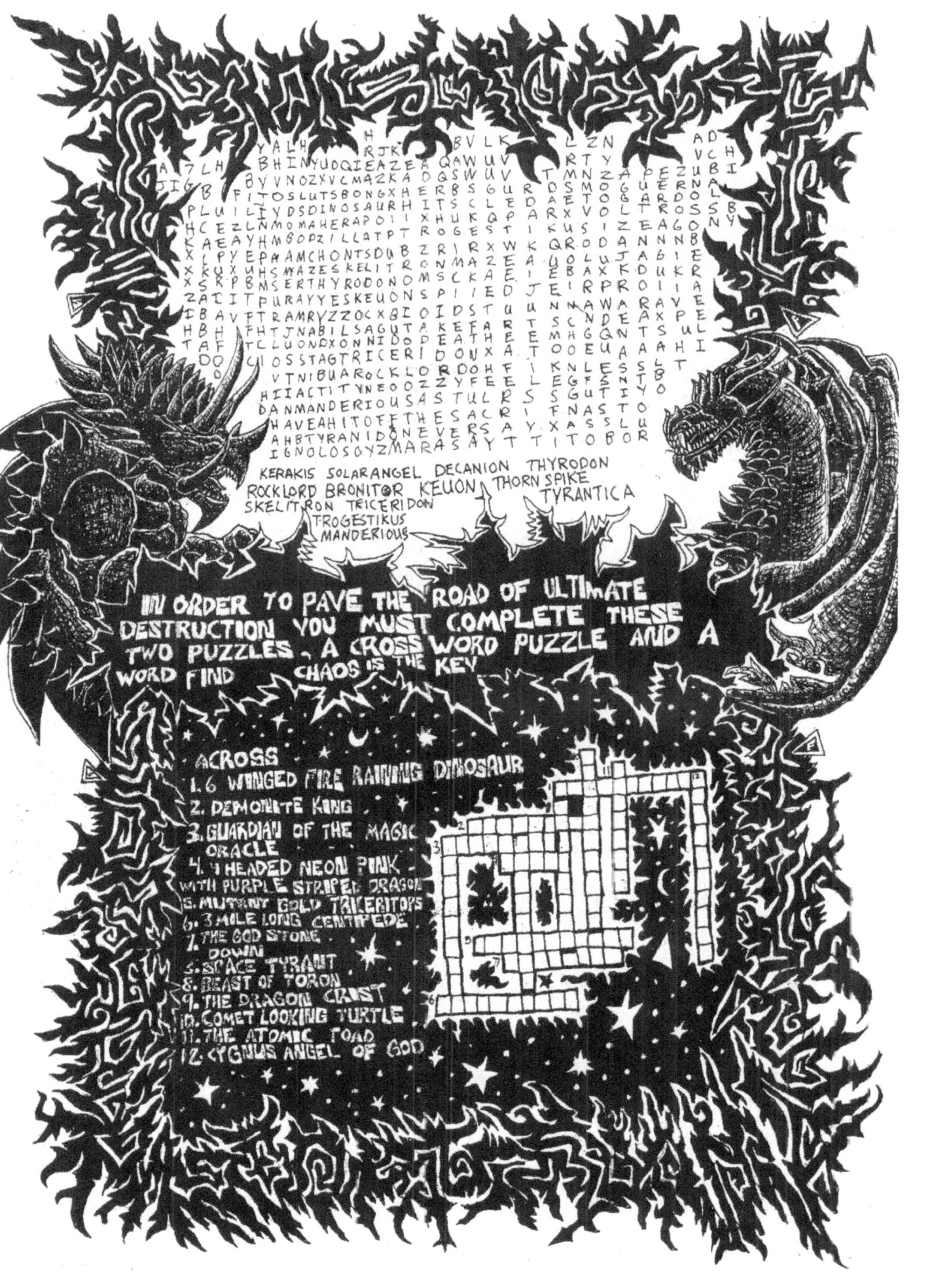

KERAKIS SOLARANGEL DECANION THYRODON
ROCKLORD BRONITOR KEUON THORN SPIKE TYRANTICA
SKELITRON TRICERIDON
TROGESTIKUS
MANDERIOUS

IN ORDER TO PAVE THE ROAD OF ULTIMATE
DESTRUCTION YOU MUST COMPLETE THESE
TWO PUZZLES. A CROSS WORD PUZZLE AND A
WORD FIND   CHAOS IS THE KEY

ACROSS
1. 6 WINGED FIRE RAINING DINOSAUR
2. DEMONITE KING
3. GUARDIAN OF THE MAGIC
   ORACLE
4. 4 HEADED NEON PINK
   WITH PURPLE STRIPED DRAGON
5. MUTANT GOLD TRICERITOPS
6. 3 MILE LONG CENTIPEDE
7. THE GOD STONE
DOWN
5. SPACE TYRANT
8. BEAST OF TORON
9. THE DRAGON CRIST
10. COMET LOOKING TURTLE
11. THE ATOMIC TOAD
12. CYGNUS ANGEL OF GOD

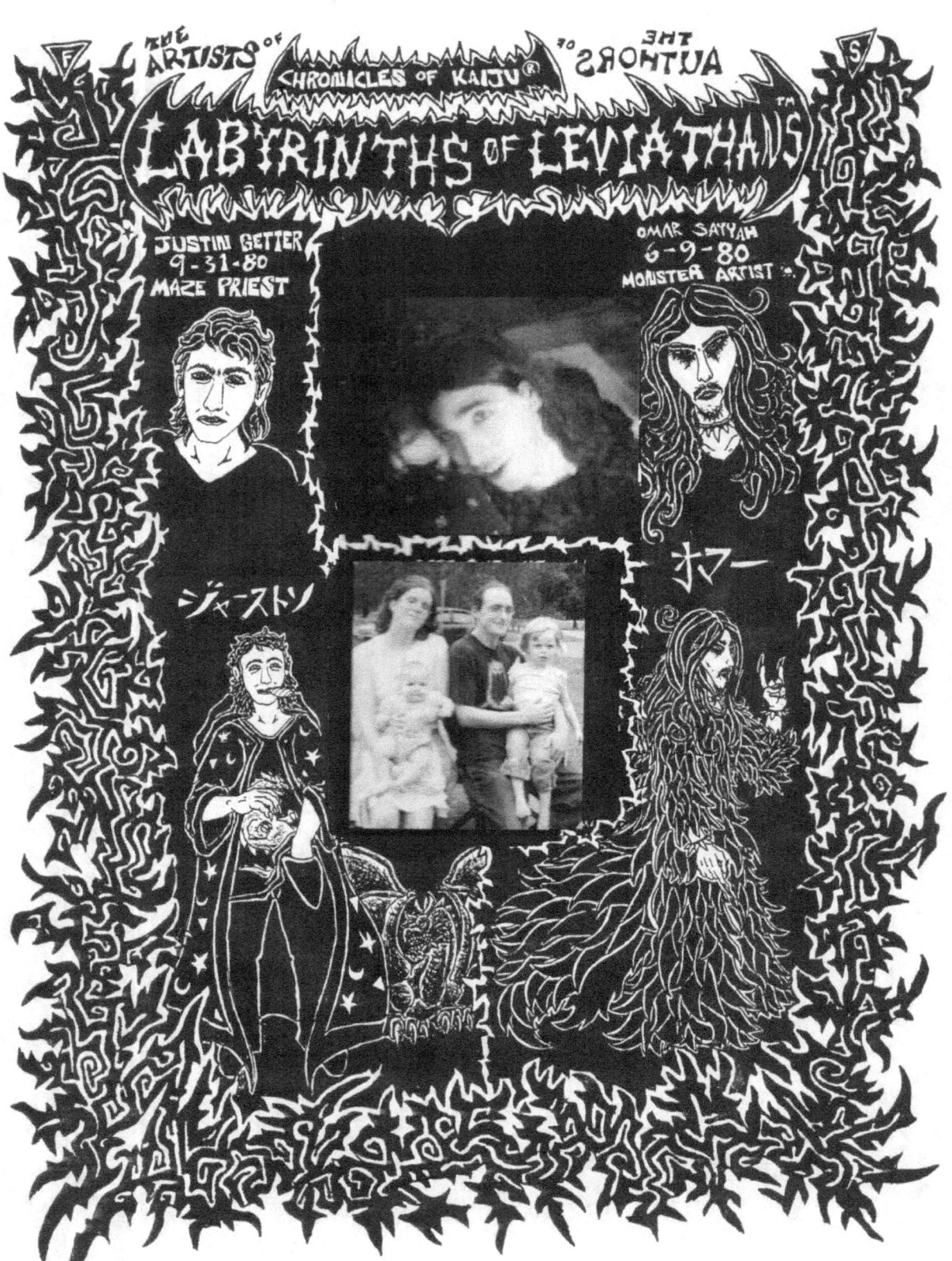

THE ARTISTS OF CHRONICLES OF KAIJU® AUTHORS OF

LABYRINTHS OF LEVIATHANS™

JUSTIN GETTER
9-31-80
MAZE PRIEST

OMAR SAYYAH
6-9-80
MONSTER ARTIST

ジャーストン

オマー

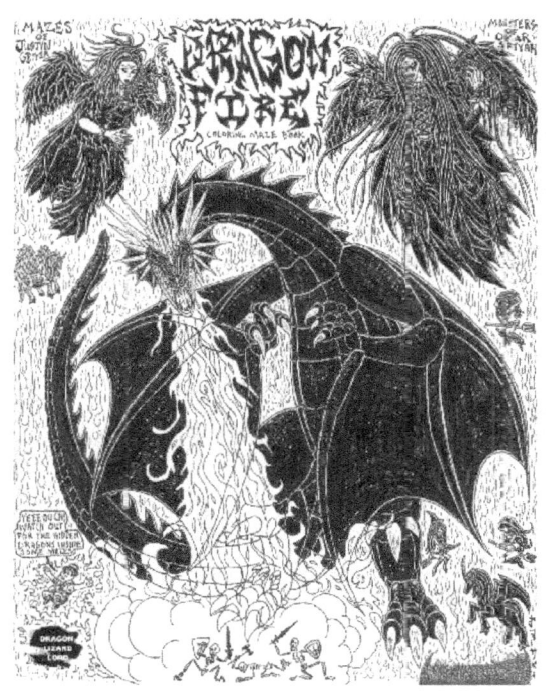

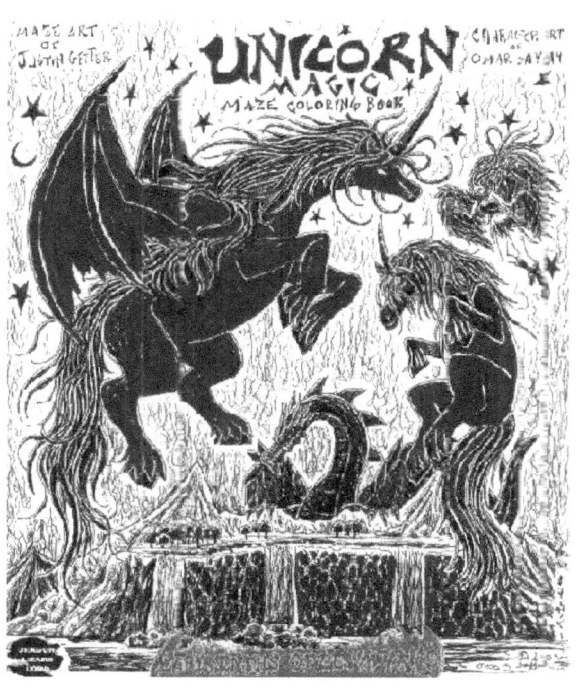

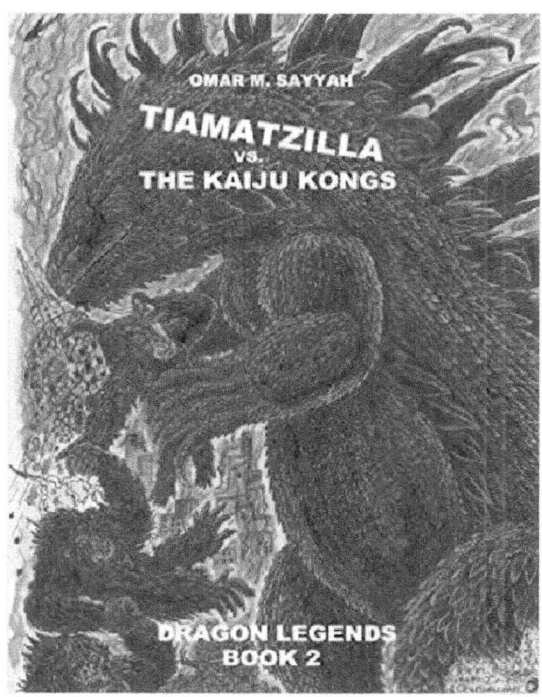

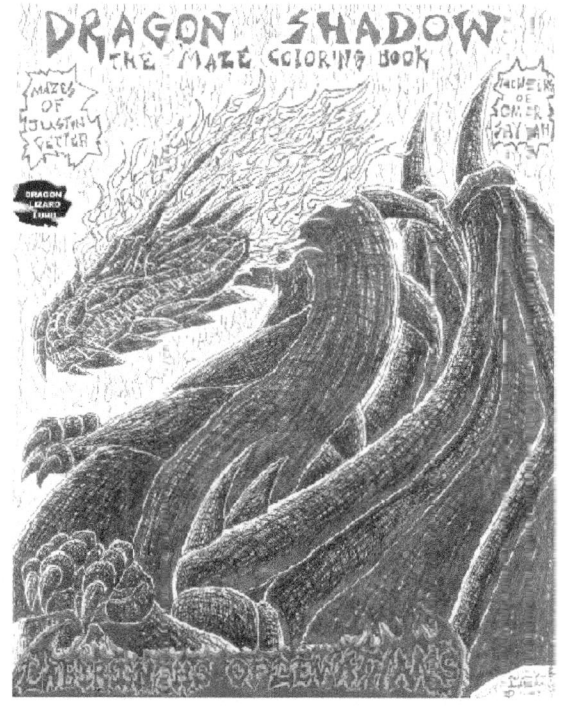